A DOG
FOR LIFE

N. GLENN PERRETT

A DOG FOR LIFE

THE PRACTICAL GUIDE TO CANINE CARE

HOUNSLOW

A Dog for Life
The Practical Guide
to Canine Care

ISBN 0-88882-134-4

Publisher: Anthony Hawke
Editor: Dennis Mills
Designer: Gerard Williams
Compositor: Robin Brass Studio
Printer: Best Gagné Book Manufacturers

Recommendations made in this book only serve as guidelines
to assist the reader in maintaining a healthy and happy pet.
Specific health care decisions regarding your pet
should be made in consultation with your veterinarian.

Publication was assisted by
the Ontario Ministry
of Culture and Communications

Hounslow Press
A Division of Anthony R. Hawke Limited
124 Parkview Avenue
Willowdale, Ontario M2N 3Y5

Printed and bound in Canada

To my parents, Helen and Norman Perrett,
whose love and understanding
were instrumental in developing my beliefs;
to my wife, Lynn,
whose love and understanding
allow me to work for these beliefs;
and to all the dogs
with whom I have had the pleasure and good fortune
of sharing my life.

Contents

Protecting Your Dog

A Dog for Life

Foreword

The attitude towards nature exhibited by the Reverend Cotton Mather, the Salem witch burner, is still prevalent today within the psyche of a great many people and is especially to be noted in the way that such individuals treat animals. One would think that after all these centuries, all humans would have learned that the other lifeforms with whom we share our planet are entitled to the same respect and good treatment that we wish to have meted out to ourselves.

There are, of course, many people who truly love animals and who share their lives with them, but some people believe that they are superior to all other forms of life and that, therefore, they are the masters of the "beasts." This attitude is often reflected in the ways that some individuals treat their pets, especially their dogs, who are probably well cared for physically in terms of the food that they get, may be well groomed, and may have a good place in which to sleep. Otherwise, however, they are treated as slavish possessions, as status symbols, or as toys to be used for amusement at those times when the "master" or "mistress" wishes to relax. My wife, Sharon, and I deal with animals of a number of kinds on a daily basis. Often, when one or another of our non-human friends happens to be in the house at meal time and human guests are present, they are often taken aback if we feed a morsel or two of our own food to a waiting mouth.

"Oh! You feed animals from the table?"

We are often asked that question, our guests seeking to be polite, but nevertheless implying criticism, not realizing that we get as much, or more, than we give in the form of love, honesty, happiness and trust.

Another annoying comment we sometimes get at meal times from a guest who is asked if he/she would like a second helping of something from the table – a guest who really does not need another helping: "Well, I will if it's going to go to waste."

This one really annoys me. Guests in our house know from the start that we never waste food. Any kitchen extras we cannot consume ourselves are given to the animals, which means that wolves, raccoons, ravens, foxes, hares, weasels, mink, etc., etc., get a share of our own meals as well as their usual ration of the top quality foods that we buy for them.

At present we do not have a dog, but we do have two timber wolves, Tundra and Taiga (the original dogs, of course), one cougar, Teca, who was declawed by the person who bought her at five weeks of age in the United States and brought her to Canada – and therefore cannot be released – and a number of ex-guests who have returned to the wild but who still come to eat at their outdoors table and to greet us politely.

After more than 30 years of caring for animals and being taught by them to respect their needs, I know that each and every one of them requires affection, that each and every one of them needs a healthy environment and that, when entrusted to human care, they deserve to be treated like a loved companion and not like a chattel that serves only to stroke the human ego.

Dogs, who almost certainly became our earliest non-human companions, need the same affection, respect and discipline from their human friends as their wolf ancestors obtain from the family pack. Indeed, as far as a dog is concerned, his human friends are bonded to him as a pack, and in as much as a dog usually enters a dwelling as a puppy, he sees his human as the pack leader. So, it is important to note that wolves have a very well-defined sense of discipline. This does not mean, however, that "underlings" are abused. It does mean that all members of a pack respect each other, quickly make up if there has been a dispute, bear no grudges or hates, and are self-disciplined once they have received the parental training needed to become a well-adjusted pack member while at the same time retaining his or her own individuality: and make no mistake about it, every wolf – indeed every living thing – is an individual, a unique being: there are no two alike.

All of the above traits and needs have been inherited by the domestic dog!

A Dog For Life is a book that should be read by all those who have a dog, or who contemplate getting one, not only because N. Glenn Perrett knows dogs, but because he loves them, all of them, especially the eleven canines with whom he and his wife Lynn share their home.

This is a book that I am happy to recommend.

R. D. Lawrence

A Veterinarian's Note

On the bookshelves these days there are numerous texts on canine care and training, each with a different approach to their topics. This book constitutes a new approach towards giving advice and helpful hints to the canine owner. Through Glenn's refreshing anecdotes and experiences with his own dogs, we can all learn something about understanding and appreciating our best friends a little better.

I can both empathize and sympathize with many of Glenn's experiences, trials and tribulations for although the number of dogs he has exceeds mine, the total "poundage" is in my favour (as a Rottweiler breeder). Many of us who have lived with dogs will undoubtedly relate to Glenn's situation or at least can better imagine them.

Our views concerning dogs may not always be the same, but his presentation in this book leads one to think and decide for his/her own self, as it should be.

The information and advice relating to veterinary topics is well presented and factual. It highlights some of the more important aspects of health care for your dog.

On his first book endeavour I wish Glenn well, and for his continued work for the humane treatment of animals, I thank him.

P. K. St. John, D.V.M.

P. K. St. John is a veterinarian specializing in companion animals. He owns and operates the Bridgeview Animal Hospital in Niagara Falls, Ontario.

Introduction

There are several reasons why I wanted to write *A Dog For Life*, but by far the most important is that all too often dogs are not treated as well as they should be. Sure, most of us know, or have known, people who took exceptional care of their canine companion. However, for every dog that is well looked after, there are several others which are not receiving all the care they deserve.

Some people deliberately mistreat dogs; however, many people simply lack information on certain aspects of dog care. In *A Dog For Life*, I try to cover a variety of topics of importance to people lucky enough to share their lives with a dog. Some of this information is known to some people who look after a dog. Other topics are rarely dealt with in books or magazines.

Although parts of this book were researched, most of it was written out of personal experience. My parents gave a home to our first family pet, Chips, a Beagle, when I was approximately two years old. I was fortunate to grow up with Chips. After Chips died, my mother vowed not to have another dog, because of the pain and grief involved with losing a beloved pet. However, after a few years, when we were

My mother holding a young Chips.

Photo: Norman W. Perrett

presented with the opportunity of adopting a Wirehaired Fox Terrier, my mother gave in, and Brandy became a cherished family member.

Brandy lived a long life and came with me when I married Lynn and moved out of my parents' house. Prior to "leaving the nest," I acquired Amorak, a Siberian Husky, who was my roommate in university. Then Lynn and I adopted Nanaimo, a Husky cross who was scheduled to be destroyed.

Since we were married, Lynn and I have taken in several dogs who were in need of a good home and family. First to come along after Nanaimo was Winston, a Terrier cross. Next came Teddy, a German Shepherd cross followed by Gleannan, a Sheltie cross, Tasha, a Siberian Husky, Nollaig, a Shepherd/Labrador cross, Samantha, a Dachshund cross and Rhew, a Siberian Husky. While I was writing *A Dog For Life*, Lynn and I adopted Rufus, a Husky cross, and Gandalf, a Scottish Deerhound. If you are counting, you know Lynn and I currently share our home with eleven dogs!

Samantha.

Many people who acquire dogs are unprepared for the commitment and responsibility involved with raising a dog. Unfortunately, although the person's initial intentions may have been good, the relationship between dog and human often sours. In these cases the dog usually ends up a victim. Many people who no longer want their pet take the unfortunate canine to the local animal shelter or pound, where the animal's future is unsure. An unsuccessful relationship between dog and person is usually the fault of the person. People who acquire a dog on a whim or fail to do their homework prior to bringing a canine friend home are increasing the chances of an unsuccessful relationship. Unfortunately, the dog is the one which pays the price, often with its life.

In *A Dog For Life*, I will tell you of things you can expect if you decide to share your life with a dog. If you already have a canine in your life, this book will provide you with ways to improve your relationship with your dog.

Having grown up with dogs (and now living with eleven of them) I, along with Lynn, have had to make numerous changes, concessions and the occasional "sacrifices." Some of these modifications have been easy, others more difficult, but they have all been worth it.

I have deliberately avoided using the term "dog owner." Taken literally, this term refers to someone who "owns" a dog. Dogs are not property – they are sensitive and beautiful animals. People who are fortunate enough to share their lives with dogs must care for and love them, in much the same way as they would human family members. And this is how I view those canines with whom we share our lives – as family members.

This book contains just some of the knowledge I have acquired in caring for "man's best friend." In fact, the main reason I wrote this book was to increase people's knowledge about dog care and suggest how they can more efficiently and effectively share their lives with dogs – the most wonderful of creatures.

Choosing
Your Dog

1. Do You Really Want a Dog?

Many people acquire a dog without giving the decision enough serious thought. Often a person buys a dog on a whim. Impulse buying often occurs when someone sees a cute little puppy in a pet store. When these animals are displayed in a store window, more people are likely to notice and "want" the dog. Puppies and dogs kept in less than ideal environments, and dogs soon to be destroyed, are most likely to draw on people's emotions. This results in impulse buying. Many people who acquire a dog under these or similar circumstances often soon realize that they really do not want the animal.

Another less-than-ideal reason for wanting a dog is because of the breed of the dog. Many people become impressed with a breed of dog (often because they have just seen a particular dog of that breed) and, without considering all the responsibilities involved in caring for a canine, go and obtain a dog of that breed. This often occurs with breeds that are experiencing popularity. For example, not too long ago it was "fashionable" to have a Doberman Pinscher. Currently, Rottweilers and Siberian Huskies are relatively popular breeds. However, popularity should not be a basis for a decision like this.

People also obtain dogs for protection. If this is the only reason you want a dog, why not get an alarm system installed? It will require considerably less care and attention and, in the long run, will likely be much less expensive.

The major reason to share your life with a dog is because you want to. You should like dogs and the companionship they provide. You must also be willing to provide proper care for the dog that you bring into your life. Anything short of this is unfair to the dog.

Dogs are social animals. They need companionship, love and care. If you are not willing to provide these basic requirements then do not get a dog. If you can provide proper care for a dog and are sure that you want one, then by all means have a dog. Sharing your life with a canine

(Opposite) The Siberian Husky is a popular breed.

companion is one of the most fulfilling and rewarding of experiences.

2. Before Acquiring a Dog

One of the biggest mistakes you can make, once you have decided to get a canine family member, is to go right out and acquire one. This is especially true if you have never lived with a dog before.

There are many things to consider prior to selecting a dog for which you will be responsible. To increase the chances of a successful and long-lasting relationship, all aspects of dog care should be carefully and thoroughly researched.

Your budget is one of the first items which should be reviewed. Dogs are not inexpensive. You should have a good idea of the basic costs involved in properly caring for a canine. Talk to the qualified staff in a veterinarian's office as well as knowledgeable employees at a pet supply store to learn about the things your dog will require – and the costs involved. Contact your local humane society as well as friends and relatives who have dogs. They can provide you with useful information about dog care and the approximate costs involved. Reading books on dog care can also help.

Knowing the costs involved in caring for your dog under normal conditions is important, but realize that an emergency situation, such as an accident requiring veterinary treatment, can occur. It is a good idea to have money set aside for such occasions.

Once you have a good idea of the costs involved in caring for a dog (and if you still want and can properly care for a canine) you should consider some of the adjustments you will have to make. You will not be able to come and go as you please; your dog will be dependent on you for a variety of things including food, exercise and love, to name just three.

Sharing your life with a dog is a long-term commitment – often ten to fifteen years, maybe more. Before acquiring a dog, look "down the road" to see if this responsibility, now and in the future, is practical. For instance, if you are a student in high school, who will look after the dog if you decide to go on to university and cannot take your canine companion? Questions like these should be considered prior to acquiring a dog.

People living in a rented dwelling should also be cautious about acquiring a pet. Many places do not permit pets. Even if your current landlord allows pets, what will happen if you have to find another rental unit? A new landlord may not be as "open-minded" about pets. It is important to have a stable environment before taking on the responsibility of a dog.

Once all the preliminary information has been collected and you are still certain that you want and can care for a dog, the next step is to actually choose a pet.

3. Choosing the Right Dog

In choosing a dog, there are numerous things to consider, including size, age, temperament and sex. While all these factors are important, temperament (the animal's mental character) is the most important and is often overlooked. Most people want friendly and affectionate dogs – which works out well because most dogs are friendly and affectionate. It is also preferable that the dog's character fits in with that of its new family (including four-legged family members).

Purebred dogs should be acquired from reputable breeders, animal shelters or pounds.

Photo: John Rutledge

Your lifestyle and personal preference should also be considered when deciding what type of canine would be well suited to you. An older person who leads a quiet and relatively inactive life may not adjust well to an energetic, young puppy. Some people are happy with almost any dog; other people are much more selective.

Unless you have a strong preference for a particular breed of dog, your local animal shelter or pound is a good place to look for that special pet. The vast majority of dogs up for adoption in these shelters and pounds make excellent pets.

If a purebred dog is desired, learn as much about the breed as possible before acquiring one. Read books about that breed and talk to people who have a dog of the breed you are interested in. As well, find out who the reputable breeders are, contact them, and visit their facilities (make an appointment first). Ask them questions before deciding which dog is for you.

If you like a particular breed but want to provide a good home to a dog in need, contact animal shelters and pounds. If they do not currently have a dog of the breed you desire, check back or leave your phone number in case a suitable canine comes up for adoption at a later date. While purebred dogs were, at one time, rarely seen in animal shelters and pounds, this, unfortunately, is no longer the case.

Pet stores are no place to acquire dogs. Sure, the little dog in the window looks cute, and this is what pet store owners strive for. Unfortunately, many dogs in this situation are purchased on a whim and, once the excitement of owning a cute, little dog wears off, it is deposited in an animal shelter, pound or worse. Also, most pet store employees do not know a breed's characteristics like a good breeder does. How could they? Pet stores sell the breeds of dogs which are currently popular. These breeds are continually changing. Another problem with buying a dog from a pet store is that many of these animals come from "puppy mills" or puppy farms where the dogs used for breeding purposes are kept in terrible conditions.

Many people who have purchased a dog from a pet store are surprised to find out that the dog they acquired is sick.

This should come as no surprise. Because many of the dogs originate from puppy mills, where they are kept in a less than healthy environment, they are prone to disease. Combine this with the fact that many of these puppies are of poor quality breeding and have to travel great distances before ending up in the often-stressful environment of pet stores, and it is no wonder that many of these puppies are not as healthy as those puppies bred by a good breeder.

If you want a companion dog, visit your local animal shelter or pound. Most shelters and pounds have a good selection of dogs of various ages and sizes, which are waiting patiently to become part of a loving family. However, if you want a purebred dog so you'll know the animal's bloodlines and other information, obtain your canine friend from a reputable breeder.

4. Canine Dispositions: Too Precious to Waste

One night while I was watching one of our dogs being exceptionally goofy, I began thinking of how each of our dogs has a unique, interesting and friendly personality. Amorak, a Siberian Husky, was the first dog I acquired. She is extremely stubborn, independent and friendly. Amorak has graciously accepted, for the most part, every dog we have brought into our family. With Amorak you are never sure what she will do next.

Nanaimo, a Husky cross, is the friendliest dog I have known. He is not only affectionate and tolerant of other canines, but he is extremely receptive and outgoing with people.

On the other hand, Winston, a Terrier cross, is not overly friendly toward most other dogs and will not tolerate Teddy, a German Shepherd cross, at all. Winston does get along well with Amorak and Nanaimo, probably because they were already with us when we acquired him. He is affectionate with Lynn and me but is suspicious of strangers. This behaviour may be because he was probably a stray for some time (and had to look after himself) before coming into our lives.

Nanaimo.

Teddy is an extremely friendly and good-natured dog who gets along with most other dogs. He is relatively obedient – at least as obedient as our canines get!

Gleannan is an excitable Sheltie cross who is Teddy's good friend. She is extremely friendly with Lynn and me but is not very trusting of people who are not familiar to her. Gleannan is "settling down" as she matures and is an extremely intelligent dog.

As Gleannan is excitable, Tasha, a Siberian Husky, is laid back. Tasha rarely gets excited and takes most things in stride. It is only on rare occasions that Tasha shows emotion. Possessing a character "typical" of many Siberian Huskies, Tasha is very friendly, stubborn and independent.

Nollaig, a Shepherd/Labrador cross, is an extremely energetic and friendly sort who demands attention. She quickly fit into the "pack" and gets along with everyone. She is also a humorous canine who amuses me on a regular basis.

Samantha, a tiny dog, is a cross of several breeds, most notably Dachshund. She is a good example of courage and perseverance. Unable to walk for the first several months of her life due to a handicap she was born with, Samantha now gets around efficiently. Along the way, Samantha's progress was stalled due to minor injuries to her fragile legs. Her legs have strengthened considerably over the last year or so. Currently she walks and runs pretty well – although her stride is somewhat unorthodox. She also gets stiff after lying down for some time. Samantha's feisty attitude to life occasionally gets her in trouble: she mercilessly chases and bites at the other dogs. While she does this in fun, the other dogs (with the exception of Rufus and Tasha) are not amused by her "games." Tasha has been a special friend to Samantha from the day we brought the tiny dog home. Tasha patiently and gently plays with Samantha while "Sam" jumps on Tasha and bites her, with authority. Tasha's patience and gentle play were instrumental in Samantha overcoming her handicap.

Rhew, another Siberian Husky, is a very tolerant and quiet dog. Like our other Huskies, she is independent, stubborn, friendly and pleasingly "different." She is also graceful and confident. Rhew gets along with everyone in our family.

Rufus, a Husky cross, came to us as an extremely timid and thin young dog. I happened to be in the lobby of an animal shelter when a woman brought her in as a stray. Because the pathetic looking and frightened dog was not going to be put up for adoption after her impound period was over, Lynn and I decided to make room for one more, provided, of course, the dog was not claimed, which she wasn't. Rufus was an older puppy when we adopted her, and she slowly came out of her shell with some good care and special attention. She was scared of numerous things, was extremely thin, and her coat was ragged, dull and lifeless. In fact, she had to be taught how to climb and descend stairs. Rufus has taken over the title of "resident clown" from Nollaig. To call Rufus "goofy" is a definite understatement. I often break out laughting while watching the silly things that Rufus does on a daily basis and her expression can put

Photo: N. Glenn Perret

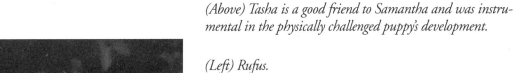

(Above) Tasha is a good friend to Samantha and was instrumental in the physically challenged puppy's development.

(Left) Rufus.

Photo: John Rutledge

me "in stitches." Rufus has become best friends with Samantha. The two dogs play together, continually and vigorously, for hours.

Gandalf, our latest (and last for some time) canine family member, is a very friendly and gentle Scottish Deerhound. He is relatively obedient and, like all of our dogs, intelligent. Our home was not Gandalf's first, it was not even his second. For some reason (or reasons) Gandalf had been in several "homes" prior to being welcomed into our family. How a friendly dog who is well behaved and affectionate can be shuttled from home to home is beyond me. Needless to say, Gandalf is a welcome and cherished family member.

It is both interesting and delightful watching our dogs develop and grow. Their personalities are unique and honourable. Each of our dogs have numerous good qualities and only the occasional "fault."

As I ponder what wonderful creatures dogs are, my thoughts turn to sorrow for all the canines who possess friendly dispositions (and even those whose dispositions are, for one reason or another, not as friendly) but will not be given the opportunity to display them. With the pet overpopulation problem, millions of these friendly canines are being destroyed annually in North America. These dogs will not get the chance to be part of a family. Their friendly, innocent and honourable dispositions will not be allowed to develop and grow as they should.

That evening, as I sat on the couch next to Amorak, Nanaimo and Nollaig (Amorak was lying beside Nollaig, with her rump literally on top of Nanaimo, who was snoozing contentedly), I had mixed feelings. I was extremely grateful to be sharing my life with eleven canines who provide considerable love, companionship, joy and affection. However, I was also very sad that so many dogs are abandoned, neglected, abused and generally treated as disposable items.

If you want to share your life with a canine, adopt a dog in need of a good home from your local animal shelter or pound. As well, if your dog is not neutered (spayed or castrated), see your veterinarian about this important procedure. The number of dogs that have to be destroyed is too many – far too many – simply because there are not enough good homes for them.

5. Mutts and Older Dogs Make Good Pets

With the pet overpopulation crisis, people wanting a pet for a companion should be looking more to animal shelters and pounds as an alternative to buying them from breeders and pet stores. You can usually acquire a nice dog at these shelters for a fraction of the price of those sold by breeders and pet stores.

This is not to say that if you really want a purebred dog you should not buy one from a breeder. On the contrary, if you do some research about good breeders and buy your dog from one of them, you will usually end up with a good dog. However, if you are not fussy as to whether the dog you get is a purebred, you might try other locations to find your "faithful friend."

If you want a particular type of dog because you have seen that breed before and like the character that breed displays, fair enough. But why not go to some animal shelter and find a dog with the characteristics you are looking for? Often a mutt has a disposition and character similar to the breeds who were responsible for its creation. For example, a few years ago Lynn and I acquired Teddy, a German Shepherd cross. His character is similar to that of German Shepherds. He is lively, faithful and, although untrained, a pretty fair watch-dog. Similarly, Winston, a Terrier cross, who came into our lives a few years back, typifies the character of many breeds of Terriers with his energetic, clever and, at times, aggressive disposition.

Occasionally, you can find purebred dogs in an animal shelter or pound. It used to be that owning a purebred dog was somewhat prestigious. Now, with the mass breeding of dogs, purebreds are commonplace and, as such, more and more are being surrendered to animal shelters, pounds and veterinary clinics. If you check for a dog in these locations, you can usually leave your name and phone number in case a dog with the characteristics you want comes in for adoption.

Unless you are very picky, you will usually find a dog you can be happy with if you visit a few animal shelters. Large animal shelters located in urban centres almost always have an excellent selection of dogs needing good homes. But your chances of finding a friendly pooch at a smaller, local pound or shelter are also good. Sometimes veterinary clinics have dogs in need of a home. A quick phone call to check if any dogs are available is worthwhile.

While puppies are cute and adorable, they are a lot of work. If you do not have considerable time to raise a puppy properly, you may want to consider acquiring a dog which

Photo: John Rutledge

Teddy, a German Shepherd cross, has a character similar to that of German Shepherds.

has already gone through the "puppy phase." However, these older dogs also require much love and attention.

A good reason for selecting an older dog is that you can usually tell its temperament. Since the dog is "all grown up," you can be pretty sure that its disposition will not change dramatically. Generally, if an older dog is well adjusted and friendly, it will remain so, provided it is not mistreated or abused.

Some people assume that dogs end up in animal shelters due to behavioural problems, but this is not the case. Unfortunately, the vast majority of dogs end up in pounds and shelters because of their guardians' ignorance or indifference.

People often venture into raising a dog on a whim, not realizing the responsibilities involved. Sometimes people acquire a dog for its appearance unaware of the animal's character. Frequently the animal's guardian is not prepared to

train the dog properly. When the dog creates a minor accident or two, the person does not have the patience to work with the animal. Taking the animal to the local pound is an easy way out. Sometimes the dog's keeper moves away or into an apartment where pets are not allowed. The result: a dog who, through no fault of its own, ends up in a shelter or pound where it may or may not be part of a family again. Other dogs end up in shelters as strays. These dogs were either abandoned or became lost and, because of a lack of identification, could not be reunited with their family. Dogs having serious flaws in their disposition are not put up for adoption. So, the dogs waiting to be adopted are usually friendly, well-behaved dogs who want nothing more than to be loved and cared for.

Of the eleven dogs in our house, two came to us as strays, three came from veterinary clinics, three came from animal shelters, one came as a puppy when her owner was no longer able to keep her, and one came from a farm. Only one came from a breeder.

Nanaimo, our first mutt, was purchased from a veterinary clinic, which had the animal control contract for the area. I had just started working part time in the clinic while attending university. Nanaimo's time was just about up, in fact if he was not adopted that day he was going to be destroyed. I could not believe it. Here was a dog no older than a year, friendly and eager to please, which was going to be killed because in the few days he was in the clinic he was not claimed or adopted.

Not satisfied with the effort to find this dog a home (actually no effort was made) I adopted Nanaimo and handed in my resignation. When I brought Nanaimo home, it was as if he knew he had been spared a terrible fate and wanted to return the favour to us by being the friendliest and most outgoing dog around. We have had Nanaimo for approximately eight years now. He is the most warmhearted dog I have ever seen.

There were other dogs at that clinic. The veterinarian who owned the clinic took on the animal control duties for the area to make some extra money. When I resigned, there was still a Doberman Pinscher, a Samoyed, and a Saluki

Photo: N. Glenn Perrett

waiting to be adopted. All were purebreds. That day, when I left, the Saluki was being killed.

All the dogs in our family have gentle dispositions. However, the dogs we acquired as strays or obtained from a shelter or veterinary clinic seem a little more "eager to please." It is almost as if they are trying to thank us for taking them in.

Of all the dogs we have taken in, five were puppies. The rest were between one and a half and five years of age. The older dogs were generally well behaved and all were housetrained. Tasha, a five-year-old Siberian Husky, who we obtained at a shelter, is not only an older dog, but she is also one of the most well behaved dogs I have come across. Not very obedient, but well behaved.

(Above) Nanaimo – the friendliest of dogs.

(Opposite) Tasha, an older Siberian Husky I adopted at an animal shelter, is an extremely gentle and well-behaved dog.

Dogs are dogs. Those that come "with papers" are not superior to those whose parents are of different breeds. They are not friendlier or healthier, nor do they live longer. As well, adopting a puppy – rather than an older dog – is not necessarily "better." If you have the time and want to go through all the stages of training your puppy, then by all means do. However, if you are not overly anxious to take on that task but want to give a dog a good home, visit your local animal shelter and give an older canine a second chance at life.

6. Multi-Pet Families

It is common for people to share their home with more than one dog. While the cost and work increase with each additional pet, these expenses usually do not increase proportionately to each new animal. Two dogs are rarely twice as much work or expense as one dog. If you have been considering acquiring a second or third dog, but are hesitant to do so, read on; the information contained in this chapter may put some of your doubts and anxieties to rest.

Prior to taking on the responsibility of another pet, you ought to carefully consider a number of things. Are you ready for the added commitment and cost? If you are not sure of the added costs involved, look into the matter. Contact your veterinarian and find out the "basics" of the veterinary care that your new family member will require and the costs involved.

In addition to the standard requirements, your pet will likely require veterinary care if it becomes sick or injured. As well, contact a qualified employee at your pet supply store to see what items your new pet will require and their approximate costs.

Buying dog food for two dogs is often cheaper per pet, provided the dogs are eating the same brand of pet food. Larger containers usually cost less per unit weight, and costs can sometimes be further reduced if you buy in bulk.

To get a reduced price, find a good manager or owner of a pet supply store who realizes it is good business to give reduced rates to those who are valued customers. So, two pets don't necessarily cost twice as much as one.

Doing your "homework" is especially important if your new pet is an animal you have not had the pleasure of caring for before. For example, the requirements and costs of feeding and providing veterinary care for a dog are different from those of a cat.

Acquiring a pet solely for company for your other animal is wrong. While this can be one reason for sharing your home with another pet, you have to want the animal and be willing and able to raise and care for it properly.

Many people use the excuse of "not enough room" for

Photo: N. Glenn Perrett

not getting another dog. These people often believe certain breeds of dogs require considerable "room to run." I have no problem with people keeping a large dog in an apartment – provided that pets are allowed in the building and the dog receives enough exercise and is well cared for. Large dogs do not require large homes. The dogs that reside in our home mostly lie around when they are in the house. They get their exercise through frequent walks and by playing in the fenced-in yard.

Besides the expenses involved with raising more than one dog, many people shy away from actually acquiring another animal because they are worried that they do not have the time to care for another pet. They feel they are already "stretched to the limit" with the time they now give their only dog. But, two dogs do not require twice as much time as one pet does. Often, the amount of time provided for one pet will suffice for two. In fact, if the first pet is frequently left alone all day, a second pet is good company – provided the two animals get along.

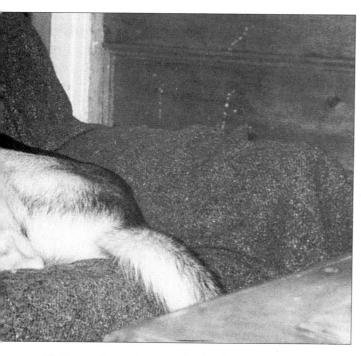

Teddy, our large German Shepherd cross, spends much of his time lying down when he is in the house.

Walking two dogs on leashes can usually be handled with little difficulty – provided the dogs have some training. Pets are often content just having you around. Our dogs are happy just snuggling on the couch while I watch television, or playing in the safe confines of the fenced-in yard while Lynn is gardening.

The only additional time required in looking after two or three pets, as opposed to one, is for activities which have to be done individually. Grooming, preparing meals, walking (if you have more dogs than you can handle on a single walk) and other activities needing a one-on-one basis do take additional time. However, having more than one pet does not take much more time unless you have many pets. For instance, the feeding process in our house for eleven dogs takes approximately twenty minutes compared to five minutes if we had to feed only one or two dogs.

If you have the time to devote to another dog, it does not necessarily mean you should acquire one. You have to want the animal and be able to afford to care for all your pets properly. Caring for one canine is a large commitment – a commitment that should be carefully thought out before obtaining the new dog.

When is enough enough? Except for municipal bylaws, contracts or other legal limitations, there are no "rules" that say when someone has too many canines. You have to decide on the number of your pets on an economic, time and emotional basis. Every dog you are raising should receive plenty of love and attention, good veterinary care, as well as the other requirements involved with raising a happy, healthy pet.

If you do not have enough money or time to spend on more dogs, then do not acquire more animals. Since I am usually at home, our dogs receive plenty of attention. In fact, Lynn's and my schedules revolve around those of our dogs! People with pets must be sympathetic to their pets' needs and requirements; these requirements include plenty of love and attention.

If a new dog is genuinely desired and will be properly cared for, another question to ask is how will your current pet(s) react to the newcomer and vice versa? While most pets get along, given time, there are the occasional exceptions. While you should already have a good idea of how your pet will react to another animal, there are ways of improving the chances of a successful introduction between animals.

Introducing a new dog to dogs or cats that have been in the family for some time can be a trying experience for both the animals and people involved. The ease with which the animals adjust to each other is dependent on numerous factors, including the disposition, age and sex of the pets involved. If two male dogs are introduced to each other and both are aggressive, there is a good chance that the two will not get along. Often, however, one of the dogs becomes dominant while the other accepts the submissive role. However, if neither animal is willing to accept the submissive role, there can be serious problems.

Unless there is a valid reason, pets should be neutered. (Females are spayed; males are castrated.) Not only are neutered pets unable to contribute to the pet overpopulation problem and are less likely to encounter numerous medical problems, but neutered pets, especially males, are likely to be less aggressive.

While characteristics such as disposition, sex, and whether or not the animal is neutered, to name but three, are important in determining the likelihood of potential problems amongst animals, how the pets are introduced to each other is also very important. Being familiar with effective ways of introducing pets to each other can make the difference between a quick and friendly adjustment period, and one which takes considerably longer and features a less-than-amiable reaction between the animals.

Once the new dog has been fully inoculated and given a clean bill of health from a veterinarian, it is alright to introduce it to other animals. Now, you have to decide on the best tactics.

Usually a slow approach is best. Some people keep the new pet confined to a room for the first while. This enables the other pets to smell it and to get used to the idea that there is another animal in the house.

When the animals are introduced, let the new dog meet the other pets one at a time. Lynn and I introduce a new dog first to the other canine family members who will readily accept the new dog.

Some people prefer to bring their established pets in to meet the new pet, as opposed to taking the new animal in to meet the other pets. Other people suggest that a more neutral territory, such as the yard, is a good location to introduce pets (which are leashed). Even if there seems to be no problems, make sure someone is with the animals for the first several days in case troubles arise. New canines in our house are kept in a separate room when we are out, until we are absolutely sure that all the dogs are getting along.

Even if all your pets get along, certain situations need a cautious approach. Feeding your pets is one such activity. Each dog should have its own food bowl and be fed well away from other pets. Make sure someone is on hand in case any altercations occur.

As well, give the resident dog plenty of attention; it may be somewhat jealous of the new "intruder." Often the resident canine thinks of itself as dominant (at least initially). If this is the case, the situation can break down if you are considerably more affectionate with the new pooch. The dominant dog, wanting to maintain its superior status, may threaten or attack the new animal. Provide all of your pets with plenty of attention.

If you are considering making room for one more dog, don't make the mistake of assuming that your new four-legged family member will automatically adjust to its new surroundings and your other pet(s). Conversely, don't make the mistake that you and your current pet(s) won't need time to adjust to the new canine in the family. Some transition periods when bringing a new pet into a home are smooth; others are hectic, to say the least. Be prepared to make whatever adjustments are necessary.

Many dogs readily "take" to their new family; others do not. Most animals eventually settle into their new surroundings, accepting a certain position in the social hierarchy.

Similarly, some animals happily accept newcomers, while others are not so understanding. Given time, the initial opposition to new family members usually wanes; occasionally it does not.

When we acquired Winston, he was welcomed by the other dogs in our house. In turn, Winston, being the new dog on the block, got along with all the other dogs. However, when we took in Teddy, an easy-going dog, Winston barely tolerated him. Both animals were neutered shortly after we got them; however, Winston simply did not want anything to do with Teddy. The intolerance on Winston's part turned to outward aggression. All attempts to curb the tension were unsuccessful. After a couple of fights we realized other arrangements had to be made.

When Winston is with the other dogs, Teddy is kept with Gleannan in their own room (complete with couch and two comfortable chairs!) When Teddy and Gleannan are with the other dogs, Winston is kept with Nanaimo in another room.

So, with time, pets usually work out their differences.

Winston does not get along with Teddy.

Occasionally, these differences continue and may even get worse.

If you are considering adopting a dog but are not sure if it will get along with your other pets, talk to veterinarians, animal behaviourists, or knowledgeable people at a humane society. Try to obtain information from several qualified people as opposed to just one or two. You might already have a good idea as to whether your current pet(s) would accept a new dog. Similarly, the people currently looking after the dog you are considering adopting will likely know how the animal responds to other pets.

Owning more than one pet can occasionally result in some trying times but, by and large, the rewards are both numerous and substantial. Making room for an "unwanted" or stray pet is an especially gratifying experience.

7. How Many is Too Many?

When are there too many dogs in a family? Good question. Some people believe Lynn and I have too many dogs. Eleven dogs in a family are more than "normal," but a variety of factors dictate how many dogs can be properly kept. There are two important questions: how much time and attention can you give your dogs? and, can you afford to care for your dogs well?

I purchased my first dog, Amorak, from a breeder. I did this when Brandy, the "family" dog, was the only other dog around. I acquired Amorak because I wanted a Siberian Husky. Before Lynn and I married and moved into our own house with Brandy and Amorak, we adopted Nanaimo, who was a stray in the local pound. Nanaimo was scheduled to be killed. All of the dogs we have since adopted were in need of a good home.

Each time Lynn and I made the decision to accept one more dog into our family, we did so only after discussing the situation and realizing that we could adequately care for one more dog and that the newest canine would not detract from the care of the other dogs. With the addition of Gandalf, Lynn and I made the decision that eleven dogs was our limit!

We took on the responsibilty of caring for so many dogs largely because most of these dogs were in need of a good home. Unfortunately, while there are numerous other dogs in need of good homes, we feel that to take in more dogs would not be fair; caring for additional animals would mean less care and attention for our current canine family.

Before taking on so many dogs, Lynn and I had to ensure that we could spend enough quality time with our dogs, daily. Obviously, with the addition of each dog, there was less time to give to the other canines. To offset this, we have had to make more efficient use of the time we give to our dogs and borrow some time we gave to other activities. While Amorak received more walks when she was the only dog in the picture, she still receives regular walks and has numerous "brothers" and "sisters" to play with inside the safe confines of the fenced-in yard.

Photo: N. Glenn Perrett

In order to spend an appropriate amount of time with our dogs, we have had to modify our lifestyle and schedules. We would not have taken in so many dogs if our schedules did not permit us considerable latitude. I am fortunate to have a job that enables me to work at home occasionally. I am also able to take one of our dogs into work. As well, Lynn's job enables her to be home late in the afternoon. So, combined with the fact that Lynn and I spend virtually every weekend at home, our dogs are not left without human companionship for extended periods of time. The time our dogs are left on their own allows our normally energetic canines some "quality" sleep.

To increase the time spent with our dogs, Lynn and I allow four dogs to sleep in our bedroom. Amorak is permitted to sleep with us because she has slept in my room since she was six weeks old – before I married Lynn! Nanaimo is also allowed to follow us to bed. Nanaimo was the third dog on the scene (after Brandy and Amorak) and was initially used to being with us before so many adopted "siblings" were around. Winston and Gleannan also sleep with us.

Sharing a bedroom with four dogs can be inconvenient at times – especially when all four canines decide to try to find an open space on the bed. However, when Amorak, Nanaimo, Gleannan and Winston snuggle with us on the bed during cold winter nights the extra warmth is appreciated. During warmer weather the dogs are more apt to sleep on the couch or the cooler hardwood floor.

Frequent activities Lynn and I share with our four-legged family members include walks on our twenty-five-acre hobby farm, grooming and playing in the fenced-in yard. Quiet time often includes sitting on the couch with the dogs while we are reading or watching television.

Because all of our dogs are "indoor" canines and our schedules revolve around our animals and home life, it is relatively simple to ensure that we spend enough time with our dogs. The only difficult task is making sure that all our

Lynn and I decided that, with the addition of Gandalf, a Scottish Deerhound, eleven canines was our limit.

dogs receive enough one-on-one attention. To do this, Lynn and I will occasionally take one dog with us into the living room, which is normally off limits to the dogs. But there is a limit to the number of dogs you can give adequate love and attention to. Our limit is eleven.

Cost is another factor that indicates how many dogs can be properly cared for. Feeding your dog with a quality dog food, providing bowls, collars, leashes, etc., and ensuring it receives adequate veterinary care is costly. All of our dogs are well fed and cared for. Annually, they receive their vaccinations and are checked for heartworm and put on a preventative program. All eleven of our dogs are also neutered. Other veterinary care and pet care items that are required are obtained.

Dogs need both a time commitment from their human family members, and a financial commitment. Both of these should be carefully considered before taking on the responsibility of raising a canine family member.

Lynn and I decided to live with eleven dogs not only because we have the love, desire, dedication and knowledge to take care of these wonderful animals, but also because we have the time and money to raise them properly. The fact that these dogs needed a good home also influenced our decision.

8. Dogs Rarely Make Good Christmas Presents

Every year the festive season results in numerous dogs being given as Christmas presents – a gift that the person on the receiving end will not soon forget. Often, the special gift is remembered for a long time, but not always with fond memories. While intentions may have been honourable, the ending is often sad, with an innocent dog as the victim.

There are several reasons why a dog is often not a good idea for a Christmas (or any other kind of) present: the animal is selected by someone other than the eventual companion; dogs are sometimes "pushed" on someone; and the surprise element is the only thing considered.

To ensure that the gift will be loved and cared for, the person receiving the "gift" should select the dog he or she prefers. Don't surprise the person with an unwanted pet. For example, if a child has its heart set on a larger Shepherd or Retriever-type dog, then that child may be disappointed if presented with one of the toy breeds.

This disappointment could result in the person never warming to his or her pet. This is unfair to the animal; it will sense that it is not really wanted. Often, these unwanted dogs are taken to the local animal shelter or pound where their future is unsure. All of this results in stress for the unfortunate animal, which has not even been given a chance.

A dog often has trouble adjusting to its new home if the festive season brings a hectic atmosphere into the house. A pet in new surroundings requires considerable attention and affection if it is to adjust quickly and successfully to its unfamiliar new home. If an animal is suddenly thrown into a disorganized setting and forgotten in some corner, it will have a more difficult time adapting. Problems in getting used to a new home inevitably place more stress on both the pet and its new family. What everyone should want is a smooth transition.

Giving someone a dog is giving someone a long commitment. Depending on the animal's age, the new guardian may be responsible for its well-being for up to fifteen years – maybe more. This has to be taken into account. For example, if a pet is being given to someone in school, who will care for the animal if the person decides to go on to college or university? Planning is important before aquiring a dog. After all, a pet is for life!

The cost involved with raising a pet cannot be overlooked. Proper care for a dog is an expensive undertaking. Dog food and other items such as leashes, collars, bowls and toys are not cheap. These costs, combined with veterinary expenses, can account for a chunk of the household budget.

Dogs should receive a veterinary examination annually, at which time it will be given the necessary vaccinations. You can count on these costs. Other veterinary expenses will depend on how healthy the animal remains over the years. A call to your local veterinarian should provide you with a

18

general idea of what your pet will require and approximately how much it will cost.

Calculate the expenses involved with properly caring for your "gift."

When these considerations have been carefully reviewed, a dog can make a good Christmas gift. But remember, to ensure a good beginning, the dog's new guardian should select his or her own pet and provide it with plenty of affection.

One way to avoid some of the problems associated with bringing a dog home at Christmas is to allow the prospective guardian to choose the animal he or she wants at a more appropriate time. Often a week or two before Christmas – or waiting until after the holiday season is over – is a more suitable time for welcoming a new member into the family. In this way, the animal can begin adjusting to its new home and family in a more normal environment. The people responsible for the canine's care will likely have more time to give the love and attention the dog will need during this settling-in period.

A practical alternative to bringing a dog home as a Christmas present is to wrap items the new pet will need and put them under the tree. The prospective "parent" will be surprised and happy knowing he or she will be able to choose a pet in the near future. This approach is practical because the necessary pet products will be present when the new member of the family is brought home.

A partial list of products for dogs include the following: dog food (puppy food), bowls, collar, leash, dog biscuits, brush, toys, identification tag.

Another good idea for surprising someone at Christmas without actually presenting an animal is giving a card indicating that a pet to be personally selected will be purchased as a present. Books on dog care also make practical Christmas gifts.

If you do your homework, know your responsibilities, and carefully prepare for the selection of a dog, the person who will look after and love the dog will be rewarded with the love and trust of a faithful friend. And that is the best gift.

9. What's in a Name?

Naming a pet can be difficult. Some people choose a name that their pet will quickly learn and respond to. Often the animal's guardians give their pet an original, distinguished and significant name that applies to the animal's character.

Lynn and I have had to come up with numerous names for our canine family. Here are some methods we used.

The first dog that I was totally responsible for was Amorak. I purchased Amorak, a Siberian Husky, from a breeder when she was six weeks old. I chose the name Amorak while reading the book *Never Cry Wolf,* by Farley Mowat. Amorak is an Inuit word meaning "Spirit of the Wolf." Resembling a small wolf and possessing considerable character and spirit, not to mention a wonderful howl, I felt the name fitted. It was also not too long, so Amorak would quickly adjust to her new name.

(Opposite) Dogs are sentient creatures, not items to be thoughtlessly given to surprise someone at Christmas.

(Below) Amorak.

Photo: John Rutledge

Nanaimo, a Husky cross, was the first dog Lynn and I acquired together. I was impressed with this dog's extremely outgoing and friendly disposition. In fact, Nanaimo is the friendliest dog, to both other dogs and people, I have had the pleasure of meeting. Naming Nanaimo just "happened." Lynn and I were discussing the proper name of those chocolate squares which have a creamy filling. Lynn argued that the proper name of these delicacies was New York squares. I disagreed: the name of the sweets was Nanaimo bars. The name Nanaimo seemed to apply to the handsome black-and-white dog with the large ears and long, feathery tail.

The next dog Lynn and I acquired was Winston, a Terrier cross. I found Winston on a hot spring afternoon, a piece of rope dangling from his collar. Winston was both scared and lost. For two days Lynn and I tried to catch the scared dog before we were able to entice him with some cooked steak and cheese. All attempts to find Winston's owners were unsuccessful. Since we found him in Churchill, Ontario, the name Winston seemed appropriate.

The next dog was Teddy, a large Shepherd cross. Because of his size and gentle disposition, we thought the reference to a large teddy bear made an apt name.

Gleannan, a Sheltie cross, became the next welcome addition to our family. The naming of dogs was becoming more difficult, so I purchased a Gaelic-English dictionary.

While leafing through the pages, I found the name Gleannan, Gaelic for "a little glen" – a nice name for a pretty dog with fine features.

Our next dog was another Siberian Husky. Since Tasha was already five years old and had had two previous owners, we felt we should not change her name. So we didn't.

Nollaig was our next canine, and again we turned to the Gaelic-English dictionary for help. Since we had acquired the energetic Shepherd/Labrador-cross puppy just before Christmas, we opted for Nollaig, Gaelic for "Christmas." Although I liked the name, to this day Lynn does not seem sold on it.

Because Nollaig's name was primarily my idea, Lynn named the next dog – Samantha. She came to us as a four-month-old puppy with a handicap, and Lynn instantly became attached to the tiny Dachshund cross.

Rhew, a young, female Siberian Husky puppy, whose previous human guardian could no longer look after her, became our next canine. Not knowing what to call the black-and-white puppy who possessed a tremendous amount of energy and character, we again turned to a Gaelic-English book for assistance. Because of her icy blue eyes and her fondness for snow and cold weather, we called her Rhew, which means "frost, ice."

(Opposite) Winston.

(Below) Rhew.

Photo: John Rutledge

After Rhew, we adopted Rufus, a skinny, terrified and scraggly, older puppy, who was slated to be destroyed. Rufus gained her title primarily because Lynn thought she looked like a "Rufus"! However, as this initially timid dog gained confidence with her surroundings and adoptive family, she developed a resounding "roof" for a bark. So her name is appropriate.

Our "newest" dog (and our last for some time) was Gandalf, a three- or four-year-old male Scottish Deerhound. This slender, distinguished looking, black dog with a grizzled muzzle resembled a wizard, so we decided to name him Gandalf, after Tolkien's admirable character in *The Hobbit* and *The Lord of the Rings*.

Names are important for everyone. It is the title by which we are known for life. So, you should select an appropriate name for those family members which are animals. Because each pet is unique, I prefer to give them names that are not common and which signify something important or special.

What is in a name? Plenty!

Gandalf.

Preparing for Your Dog

24

10. Being Prepared for a Puppy

Many people looking for that special canine opt for a puppy. Not only are puppies cute, they are also a lot of work and a large responsibility. People considering acquiring a puppy should be well prepared for the raising of this animal.

I have had the pleasure of raising five puppies (four of them with Lynn). Each puppy had its own needs while growing up. With each additional puppy, I have become a little more knowledgeable about the dog's needs and a little more prepared. By the time Nollaig came into our lives, Lynn and I were not only excited about the prospect of raising another canine family member, we were relatively well prepared!

Although we already had six dogs, Lynn and I somehow managed to come across a four-month-old, female, Shepherd/Labrador-cross puppy in need of a good home. The poor animal had been abandoned on a country road. Animal control took the "stray" to the local veterinary clinic, which also acted as the area pound. Even though she had an exceptionally friendly disposition, her holding period was soon up. Realizing that we probably had room for one more dog in our house (which we have "realized" four times since), we decided to take on the responsibility and challenge of raising a puppy one more time.

Raising a puppy is a very exciting and demanding experience. However, this task is further complicated if more than one dog resides in your house. The fact that six canines were already living in ours certainly made things interesting.

To raise the puppy properly, provide the other dogs with plenty of attention, and still maintain a relatively sane household, we had to be sure we were prepared to deal with all the inconveniences associated with bringing a new dog home.

We took the puppy, Nollaig, to our local veterinarian for vaccinations and deworming, and she was kept separated from our other dogs for about a week. This separation pe-

(Opposite) Amorak as a six-week-old puppy.

riod was necessary to ensure that Nollaig was not carrying any infectious disease, before introducing her to her new family. This period also allowed Nollaig to adjust to the new environment and allowed her time to respond to her vaccines. She was introduced to her new "brothers" and "sisters" only after the assurances of a veterinarian.

Know the basic veterinary requirements your dog will need, and the costs involved. A phone call to a cooperative veterinary office may help. As well, veterinary offices can usually provide reading material on dog care. This initial contact with a veterinary hospital may help you establish a long-lasting relationship with the facility.

Bringing the Pup Home

It is better if two people can go to pick up the puppy. While one person is busy driving, the other person can comfort the puppy on the way home. A crate (or box) should be used to confine the puppy safely, while in the car. This is particularly important if only one person is on hand to welcome the dog. Make sure the box or crate is well ventilated and that the puppy cannot get out. Old towels and other cleaning materials should be taken along as well, in case the puppy gets car sick or relieves itself.

It is also a good idea to take along a collar and leash for the puppy. An identification tag with your name, address, phone number (including the area code) and the puppy's name, should be attached to the collar. Durable, nylon collars with your dog's name and your phone number (including the area code) embroidered on the collar are useful – provided the dog does not slip its collar and the embroidered phone number remains legible. (There is more information about this in Chapter 17.)

To prepare your puppy for the trip home, take it for a walk just before departing. If it relieves itself outside, praise it.

The best time of day to bring a puppy home is in the morning, so the dog will have plenty of time to explore its new surroundings in the daylight. The more settled the puppy becomes with its new environment during the day, the less it will miss its old family at night.

When you get the new canine home, take it for a short walk around the property. Again, if the dog relieves itself outside, praise it. Show it where it will be staying indoors. Introduce it to its water and food bowls and its new sleeping quarters. Do your best to comfort the puppy and make it feel at home. While this is an exciting and anxious time for both of you, the puppy is bound to feel somewhat disoriented and alone with its new surroundings – especially with no brothers or sisters for moral support! You might want to confine the puppy to a small area of the house, a room or two, at first so it will not be overwhelmed.

Now that your puppy is home, it is time to give it a name. The shorter the name the quicker the puppy will learn and respond to it. At first the puppy will seem puzzled by the funny sound you keep saying. However, if you repeatedly call your puppy by name, it will soon identify itself with that strange new sound.

Keeping the Pup "Safe"

Since puppies and trouble are synonymous, have a "trouble free" location for the dog when you are not in the same room with it. Since Nollaig was only four months and already forty pounds, we selected a large crate – forty-eight inches long by thirty-six inches high by twenty-six inches wide. The crate provides a secure place for Nollaig when we cannot keep an eye on her.

Besides keeping the puppy out of harm's way, the crate also provides the dog with a secure environment in which to seek shelter, if the "outside world" becomes too much.

In order to get Nollaig used to her very own space, we tried to get her to associate her crate with good times. This involved feeding her in her crate. When she was tired, we would crate Nollaig with a pressed, rawhide bone that she could chew on before falling asleep amongst her blankets.

Another important reason for crating Nollaig during meals was that it provided her with a safe place to dine. Bringing a new dog into a house of dogs is sure to upset the equilibrium somewhat. Increased tension is evident mostly at feeding time. The aggressive nature of a couple of our dogs could have resulted in a fight over Nollaig's food.

Nollaig takes an "after dinner" nap in the safe confines of her crate.

On the other hand, a fight can occur if an unwary puppy goes near other dogs while they are eating. It is best to let the puppy get fully acquainted with the other canine members of the family before allowing it to eat in the same room with them. Make sure someone is present in case any problems occur.

Putting Nollaig in her crate at happier times made night time (and when she was left alone) much easier. If a dog is only crated as punishment or when it is left alone, it will associate the crate in a less-than-positive way.

Although Nollaig did not spend much time in her crate, it was worthwhile knowing that there was a place where we could put her that was "worry free." Even when we were keeping an eye on her outside her crate, Nollaig would often escape our sight and get into trouble, as only puppies can. One time I found her chewing an expensive pine hutch. After a light scolding I went back to what I was doing. Within a few minutes I heard her noisily chewing the couch. As the job I was doing was fairly important, I put Nollaig in her crate with several of her allowable toys.

Now that Nollaig has become accustomed to her crate, she voluntarily goes there when she is tired of playing or simply wants a secure spot, away from the other dogs. She just curls up with a good, pressed, rawhide bone.

Choosing Items for Your Pup

Besides the crate, other important items we purchased included water and food bowls, collar (with identification), leash, brush, chew bones (to be given under supervision), toys, books on dog care and materials for cleaning up any accidents.

The best bowls are of stainless steel. They are not only the most sanitary, but also the easiest to clean and the most durable. Do not use bowls made of pottery with lead glazes. These are poisonous.

Before your puppy is fully grown, you will have to adjust its collar from time to time; however, adjustable collars only adjust so much. Check your puppy's collar often to see if it needs adjusting or if a new one is required. A strong leather or nylon collar is good. A collar that fits properly allows you to fit two fingers between the collar and the dog's neck but will not be loose enough to pull the collar over the dog's head. Check the collar frequently; puppies grow quickly. As well, the collar might become too tight if the dog grows a winter coat. A choke chain is not appropriate as an everyday collar; it should be used only during training sessions. The leash should be strong and durable.

Some toys are not safe. Check with your veterinarian and the pet supply store employee to see what toys are appropriate for your puppy. In general, soft plastic toys which are easily chewed apart and "squeaky" toys, where the "squeaker" is easily removed, should be avoided.

Good books on dog care offer valuable information. If you read some of these before obtaining a puppy, you will be better prepared in raising a good dog successfully.

Making Your Home "Safe"

Before your puppy comes home, make sure that your house and yard have been "dog proofed." This involves removing, or making inaccessible, any objects inside and outside the house that can harm your pet.

Outside, things such as pieces of broken glass, nails and pieces of metal should be removed. Electrical wires, both inside and outside the house, should be made inaccessible.

Toxic substances – pesticides, solvents, cleaning materials and other chemicals – should be safely stored away. Substances such as ethylene glycol, present in anti-freeze and brake fluid, should be cleaned up immediately and thoroughly if spilt.

Many house and outdoor plants are poisonous to pets. Indoor plants such as philodendrons, diefenbachias and poinsettias, to name but three, should be placed out of reach of the inquisitive puppy. (See Appendix A.)

Until your "best friend" is house trained, you might want to remove carpets in those rooms your puppy frequents. Also, because your puppy will tend to chew "everything," don't leave anything around that you value.

Ensure that outside doors are not opened unless your puppy is safely confined and cannot make a dash to the outside world.

Have a safe area outside for your dog. If you take your dog for several walks daily and do not let it outside other than for its walks, then this area is not needed. However, if you only walk your dog once a day, you should have a space where your dog can exercise safely. Ideally this area will be a fenced-in yard from which your canine cannot escape.

A well-constructed pen also provides an appropriate area for your dog when it is outdoors. If your dog spends considerable time outside, it will need a good doghouse for shelter from the elements. A non-spillable water dish is also required.

Holding Your Pup
If this is the first time you have raised a puppy, the proper way to pick up and hold a pup is by placing one hand under its chest and the other under the puppy's rear end. Children should also be taught this, as well as when and how to play with the puppy – and when to leave it alone.

Training Your Pup
If the puppy relieves itself indoors, which it is bound to do, do not harshly scold it. The puppy is excited; often these mishaps are caused because the puppy is nervous and anxious. Gently scold the puppy if you catch it in the act, by gently tugging on the "scruff" of the puppy's neck and saying "no" – and then immediately taking it outdoors. Praise it when it relieves itself outside. Remember though, many young puppies cannot contain themselves, certainly not throughout the night. As well, do not discipline the dog if some time has passed after it has relieved itself indoors. The dog will not associate its mistake with the scolding, if the wrongful act occurred an hour earlier. Around three months of age, puppies are better able to control their natural functions. After meals and naps, the puppy should be taken outside immediately. Praise it when it relieves itself outdoors.

If you have another dog, the puppy will have to be introduced carefully, especially if both dogs are male. During the first few hours after the puppy arrives home, both dogs should be kept on a leash. As well, both should be fed separately for the first few days. Later on, both dogs can be fed in the same room but from different bowls spaced well apart. Make sure someone is nearby in case trouble develops.

Give the resident dog plenty of attention, since it is likely to be somewhat jealous of the new intruder. Usually, the established dog will think of itself as dominant, and the puppy willingly accepts the submissive role (at least until it grows up a little). This situation can break down if the owner is considerably more affectionate with the new puppy. The dominant dog, wanting to maintain its superior status, may threaten or attack the puppy. You can usually rectify this situation by giving more attention to the established dog.

When Nollaig was brought home, she accepted the submissive role readily, rolling over on her back when the other dogs approached. The fact that she was female and very friendly certainly helped her to be accepted quickly into the "pack."

The first night or two will likely be difficult for your puppy. This is particularly true if your puppy is quite young and has never been away from its family. The puppy will miss its mother and siblings most at night.

Perhaps the most humane approach to this problem is to place the puppy in a crate and let it sleep there. Although several nights may be noisy, the puppy should adjust quickly to its crate if some of the "comforts of home" are present. Clean blankets, a dog biscuit and a safe toy or two are items the puppy will appreciate. If a puppy is "exhausted" after an hour or two of play just prior to bedtime, you may get a more restful night.

Feeding Your Pup
During the first few days, your puppy should be fed the same puppy food that it was used to eating. Changing its food right away, combined with all the excitement, will likely result in your puppy vomiting or having diarrhea. Find out which food it is used to and have some on hand when you bring the puppy home.

If you want to change your dog's diet, add a little of the

new food to its usual diet, then slowly increase the proportion of the desired dog food until the puppy is only eating the dog food you have selected for it.

Since the nutritional requirements for puppies are different from those of mature dogs, buy a quality puppy food. Your veterinarian will help you in selecting the proper food, as will the qualified personnel of a specialized pet food store.

Protecting Your Pup

After acquiring your puppy, you should take it immediately to a veterinarian for a checkup. Be sure to take a fecal sample from the puppy to be analyzed. Also, take any information about the dog's history with you, such as previous health or vaccination records.

Work out a suitable vaccination schedule for your puppy with your veterinarian. The schedule will vary, depending on the age of the puppy.

It is a good idea to keep your puppy close to home and away from other animals and people until it has had all the necessary vaccinations. People want to "show off" their new puppy, but puppies are extremely susceptible to disease. Until your puppy has been fully innoculated, extreme care should be taken where your puppy goes. For example, avoid high-risk places such as dog shows and kennels. Avoid areas frequently used by other dogs and their guardians. Disease can be transmitted in a variety of ways, including direct contact with other animals and people. Frequenting areas where infected animals have been can also result in your puppy contracting a disease. Viruses can be transmitted through the air. So, until your puppy has had all of its vaccinations, resist the urge to display it.

Socialization with people is very important when pup-

Nollaig (approximately five months old) relaxes on the couch.

pies are between the ages of eight and sixteen weeks. Social-izing your puppy while protecting it from disease is a fine line to follow. However, common sense, educating yourself about the various diseases your puppy can contract, and knowing how to reduce the chances of your puppy being infected will greatly improve your chances of raising a healthy puppy.

Once your dog has been fully inoculated, you can start socializing it with both people and other canines. A good way to accomplish this is to take it to an obedience club. These clubs, which offer puppy and novice levels, benefit both you and your dog. You will learn the proper way of handling and controlling your dog, as well as what good care entails. The dog will learn (hopefully) what it can and cannot get away with. Obedience to simple commands such as "come" and "stay" could save your dog's life one day. As well, dogs taken to obedience school become socialized with numerous other dogs and people. You do not want a dog that is afraid of people. All of this leads to a better behaved dog and a more-informed human companion.

Raising a puppy is demanding. Patience and understand-ing, two valuable characteristics, will help you through this period. Doing your homework and properly preparing for your canine companion are your responsibilities.

Raising a good dog and cherished family member is a large undertaking. It is also a very special and rewarding ex-perience. For after the cute and awkward stage of puppy-hood, your young canine will develop into a faithful friend whose character is, by and large, honourable.

11. Making Sacrifices for Your Dog

The term "sacrifice" is a little strong, but once you bring a dog into your family, you are responsible for the animal's well-being.

Your dog will require food, water and exercise, daily. As well, you should provide your dog with some "quality time" every day. You may have to change your schedule, but re-sponsibly caring for a dog requires time. You cannot go away for a weekend and not take your dog, or without mak-ing arrangements for a responsible person to take good care of your dog.

Besides providing various items to ensure your dog's well-being, you will have to adapt to changes in your dog from time to time. When Brandy, our Wirehaired Fox Terrier, grew old, she had the occasional indoor "accident." Brandy urinated on the floor, and while it was inconvenient for us, it was also understandable, and Lynn and I realized that some changes were needed. To minimize Brandy's disability we tore up the carpeting in the family room where Brandy spent much of her time and put down flooring that could be easily cleaned. Brandy kept warm and comfortable by sleeping on a bed Lynn had made for her. This was only one of several minor changes Lynn and I had to make to suit our dogs.

Another change involved constructing a fenced-in yard for our dogs when we moved to a new house (which has thankfully only occurred twice). The fenced-in area pro-vides a safe environment in which our dogs can play and get some exercise.

Growing animosity between Winston and Teddy re-sulted in our having to separate the two dogs permanently. Over time their intolerance of each other grew from the oc-casional growl to the odd scuffle to nasty fights. Although the two fighting dogs were quickly separated and did not injure one another, Lynn and I did receive some bites and scratches while playing the role of peacemakers. After a cou-ple of these incidents, we decided to keep Winston and Teddy apart.

Having to separate the two dogs was an inconvenience: they would have to be fed separately and be allowed in the fenced-in yard at different times, etc. But there was no other solution; they were both a large part of our lives and our family.

Separating the two dogs was a more humane solution than trying to find a new home for either of them. Teddy stays part of the day in his own room along with Gleannan,

(Opposite) As Brandy grew old, changes had to be made for her.

31

who always gets along well with the large Shepherd cross and keeps him in line! The two dogs have their own couch and each has a comfortable chair. When Teddy and Gleannan are with the other dogs, Winston and Nanaimo stay in another room. This way all the dogs spend considerable time with Lynn and myself and also have canine companionship.

The animosity between Teddy and Winston is a little inconvenient, creating slightly more work for Lynn and myself, but we took on the responsibility of caring for these two dogs. While separating the two dogs is not ideal, it is an amicable solution we can all live with quite nicely.

With eleven dogs in our family (plus four horses, a donkey and four cats) Lynn and I do not get the chance to go away together. If we do decide to have a short holiday we take separate vacations – and the person on holiday takes along a dog or two! While separate vacations are a slight inconvenience, the joy the dogs provide is immeasureable. The minor "sacrifices" we have to make are nothing compared to the numerous and varied positive things we receive from our dogs.

Raising a dog is a large responsibility. Quality dog food, veterinary and other necessary expenses can be significant items in the household budget. These expenses, along with the time required to raise a canine family member properly, are necessary. However, the friendship, unquestioning loyalty and companionship that a dog provides are worth these "sacrifices" – and more!

12. Indoor vs. Outdoor Dogs

Should a dog be kept primarily indoors or outdoors? This is a valid question, particularly for those people considering acquiring a dog for the first time. Some people would not think of allowing a dog in their house. Others firmly believe that their pets are entitled to live with them.

Lynn and I believe that canine family members should be treated similarly to their human guardians, allowed to play and exercise outdoors safely, but also to enjoy the comforts of living inside the family dwelling.

Many dogs are not "outdoor" dogs. Some dogs can manage outside provided they have a good doghouse and have been acclimatized when they are younger.

An "outdoor" dog requires adequate shelter. A good doghouse should be large enough to allow the animal to stretch out comfortably. The shelter should be insulated, be impermeable to wind, have an exterior door flap, be elevated a few inches off the ground, and face away from the prevailing winds. As well, the size of the doghouse should be directly related to the size of the dog. This is important if the dog is to keep warm with its own body heat. If you are going to keep your dog outside, ensure that it has good protection from the elements. While most people associate a doghouse with winter, it is also important as shelter from the sun and intense heat of summer. In addition, all dogs should always have access to fresh water in a non-spillable container. For more information on proper care for an "outdoor" dog contact a humane society.

A major reason why I believe a dog should not be kept strictly outside is because the vast majority of these dogs receive minimal attention from their human family members. Often the "outdoor" dog only sees someone for the time it takes to place the animal's food bowl before it and give the canine "a pat on the head."

Dogs are social animals. They need love and attention. More often than not, dogs kept outside do not receive as much attention as they should. Many of these poor canines are lonely. Often, once the excitement of acquiring a puppy or dog wears off, the animal is left outside where it is virtually ignored.

Our dogs love playing and exploring in the safe confines of our fenced-in yard. And their enjoyment of the outdoors is year round. While they do spend considerable time running around the fenced-in yard or going for walks, our dogs do enjoy the comfort and companionship found within our home. They only have access to the yard when we are at home and can keep an eye on them. The dogs enjoy their

(Opposite) Many outdoor dogs lead a lonely existence.

outdoor "freedom" but they also prefer the fact that they can come inside whenever they want to. They stay inside when the weather is not to their liking. They also sleep inside, snuggling together on the couch, curling up on a warm blanket or dog bed during the colder weather, or stretching out on the cool ceramic-tile floor during the warmer weather.

The companionship and love we provide for the dogs and which is generously returned by them is easily attained because they are "indoor" canines. Lynn and I, along with our four-legged family members, spend most of our time in the family room. It is here where we can enjoy our wonderful dogs and also meet their (and our) social needs. These needs would not be as easily nor as effectively met if the dogs were kept strictly out-of-doors.

If your dog is an "outdoor" dog, at least make sure it is comfortable. A nice doghouse inside a fenced-in yard or dog run, from which your dog cannot escape, is a significant start. As well, ensure the animal receives plenty of attention. Take it for frequent walks, play with it and groom it. Better yet, try sharing your home with your dog – even in a part of your home. You will likely find that you both will benefit from this closer relationship.

13. Making Your Home Suitable for Dogs

Some reasons for having to find your animal a new home are legitimate. In the vast majority of cases, however, the poor animal has become a victim of circumstances that could have been avoided if the animal's guardians had given some thought to the potential problems ("inconveniences") – and possibly made some adjustments.

Since these tragic circumstances occur time and time again, the dog's human family should look ahead to some of the "sacrifices" they may have to make before taking on a new canine family member.

When Lynn and I moved six years ago, we knew we would have to make some adjustments. Although we made careful plans, we have been constantly making minor changes.

During the past six years we have seen our family grow from three to eleven dogs. (We have also moved, again, to a twenty-five-acre hobby farm in rural Ontario.) To make matters more difficult, two of the dogs we acquired do not like each other and have to be kept separated. In order to renovate the homes we have lived in, maintain a semi-sane household and properly raise our canine family members we have had to make adjustments.

The first job involved constructing a fence so that the dogs could play safely in the backyard. If built properly, a fence prevents dogs from gaining access to potentially dangerous situations such as roads and highways. Permitting your dog to run at large is irresponsible. Besides, in most areas, it is against the law to allow your dog to run loose.

Some people actually believe it is better to let their dogs run loose (although they may become road casualties) than to keep their beloved canines confined. Other people believe their dogs are so well trained that they would never leave the property on their own. Unfortunately, many dogs seem to forget their training once they see another dog, squirrel or similar attraction.

In order to give our dogs plenty of room to exercise, yet keep them safely away from any troubles, we knew we would have to construct a good fence. Although we had set aside enough money for the fence, by procrastinating and underestimating the time needed, we did not get the job completed before winter set in, and we had to give in when the snow began drifting in January. It was finished early the next spring.

Fencing in the backyard, approximately one hundred by sixty feet, not only provided the dogs with a large, safe area in which to play, but was also a good investment. The six-foot-high privacy fence not only kept the dogs in but it also looked nice. (For more about fences, see Chapter 14.)

Brandy was another problem. Our old Terrier was no longer able to last ten or twelve hours without relieving herself. To make matters worse, the family room (in our first home) was the main room where the dogs stayed. Being the largest room (over four hundred square feet) and having wall-to-wall shag carpet, the dogs usually resided in this room while we were at work. When it became apparent that Brandy was occasionally urinating on the carpet we realized it was time for changes.

We decided to remove the old, shag carpet, which had its advantages and disadvantages. Actually, the only advantage the carpet provided was a warm surface for the dogs to sleep on. Since the younger dogs did not mind the cooler, plywood floor and usually slept on the couch or a comfortable chair anyway, it was only Brandy who would have to endure the cooler climate (her stiff joints no longer allowed her to jump up on the couch easily).

To give Brandy a cosy place to sleep (after all she was the eldest stateswoman of the house and hence prone to sleep the day away) Lynn made a large pillow out of an old sheet.

Photo: N. Glenn Perrett

Into this she placed a generous amount of foam chips purchased from a fabric store. The pillow was then sewn shut. Lynn then made an outer case from a thicker fabric to fit over the enclosed pillow. This casing was left open at one end so that it could be easily removed and washed. This inexpensive dog bed allowed us to remove the old carpet and still provide Brandy with a warm place to sleep away the day. We have since purchased similar, commercially available pillows for some of our other dogs.

Over the plywood floor we installed an inexpensive and attractive pine floor. The floor was easy to maintain, more in keeping with our century home and, again, increased the value of our house. A wood floor is not only easier to clean than a carpeted floor, if you have pets, but it also makes flea

control easier if that problem ever arises (see Chapter 24). We put an area rug over part of the floor for the dogs to lie on. The rug can be easily rolled up and cleaned outside.

Since the family room was more of a room for dogs, where they had the run of the place, we had to make other adjustments to keep the room attractive yet practical. To prevent the dogs from damaging the walls, we added four-foot pine wainscotting to the walls. This not only finished off the family room and complimented the new floor but virtually eliminated any problems that might be caused by the dogs damaging the walls while playing. Like the floor, the wainscotting was inexpensive, easy to install and increased the value of the house.

On our current property, Lynn and I again constructed a large, fenced-in area for our dogs and renovated the family (dogs') room – keeping our canines' needs in mind. As with our previous house, wainscotting protects the walls. However, instead of a wood floor, which our dogs scratched in our first home, we installed a gray ceramic-tile floor, with a dark gray grout to help hide the dirt as well as any unfortunate accidents. The tile floor is easy to clean, extremely durable, and was also a wise resale renovation. In both homes, the family room led, via large, sliding glass doors, to the safe confines of the fenced-in yard, where our dogs spend their time outside. The biggest concern in the yard at our first home was the damage the dogs could inflict on our vegetable garden. If all our dogs were well trained there would not be a problem. We would simply show them that the vegetable garden was off limits and they would obey – right? Fat chance. Our dogs are not well trained so we tried to deter them from visiting the garden by roping off the area.

Our worst fears were soon realized. While several of our dogs were subtly destroying the garden, Nanaimo was less discreet. As soon as the tomatoes began turning red, he be-

Replacing the carpeting with wood flooring, installing wainscotting and putting down an area rug were three adjustments we made to ensure our family (dogs') room was both attractive and practical.

gan raiding the garden. Often we would find him coming out of the garden squishing a bright red tomato between his teeth. These little exploits were amusing at the time, but something had to be done. What? As soon as the ripe tomatoes were gone, Nanaimo's new habit made him turn to the green tomatoes. He was hooked! Soon our lovely garden was a shambles. Between Nanaimo searching for new adventures in canine cuisine and the other dogs playing tag amongst the vegetables, our garden was a lost cause.

Efforts to stop the dogs from causing mass destruction were hopeless. We had two choices: to construct a wood fence around the garden or to plow it under and turn the garden into lawn. We decided on the latter.

Another problem involved the dogs' destruction of the grass at the bottom of the stairs leading from the deck to the lawn. With six dogs constantly running over a grassy area, the grass soon turned to dirt which, after a rain, turned to mud, and this was being constantly tracked into the house. To reduce the dirt, we built a small flagstone patio at the bottom of the stairs. The patio was not only effective in eliminating much of the dirt the dogs brought into the house, but it complimented the transition from the wood deck to the lawn. Again, this project was easy to do and inexpensive, costing only the gas it took to drive to the country for some flat rocks.

Because Lynn wanted some kind of flower garden, we decided to try a well-placed rock garden beside the deck. We used large, jagged rocks to deter the dogs. A favourite pastime for Amorak and Nanaimo during the warmer months is to dig six inches to a foot into the cooler soil. We believed that by strategically placing large rocks in specific parts of the garden this practice of lying on and amongst the plants could be avoided. The rocks reduced, but did not eliminate, Amorak's and Nanaimo's messy, but understandable, habits. Within our present property, the fenced-in yard is rugged, consisting of a combination of trees, bushes and lawn. Although there is no garden to dig up, our Huskies excavate the lawn to lie in the cooler soil found several inches below.

Raising puppies has forced us to make minor adjustments. Since puppies are prone to chew practically any-

thing, we had to ensure that Gleannan, Rhew and Rufus were not left unsupervised in rooms that contained good furniture and other valuables (until they could be trusted). Also, anything that could be harmful to dogs, such as electrical wires and poisonous plants, were made inaccessible to all of our canines. This was done by removing the dangerous substances or putting them out of their reach and covering electrical wires with objects that could not be moved, or unplugging the wires.

Until dogs outgrow their chewing habits, they must not be left alone in potentially dangerous areas. We accomplished this by leaving Gleannan in a room that was practically empty. We also left her with Teddy for company and because Teddy and Winston have to be kept apart. Another way to ensure a puppy's safety is to crate it when it cannot be watched.

(Opposite) Tasha relaxes in the planter.

(Below) Gleannan, a Sheltie cross, is one of our friendly and affectionate canine family members who was in need of a good home.

Photo: N. Glenn Perrett

Having eleven dogs involves a fair amount of work, adjustment and compromise. However, with careful planning, education and a little foresight, changes can be worked out with a minimal amount of inconvenience. With careful planning, you can provide your pet with a comfortable and happy life while enhancing your own. Not only are all our dogs a joy to live with, but the renovations we made would probably not have occurred – at least not as quickly – were it not for our canine family members.

These are just some of the adjustments we have made to make our home more suitable for our pets. Granted, with eleven dogs, we have had to make more concessions than most people living with a canine or two would. However, even caring for a single dog will mean some changes.

Just remember, when making the necessary adjustments, make sure you like these changes (or at least can tolerate them). If you are unwilling to make any concessions, then you should not take on the responsibility of raising a canine family member.

14. Constructing a Fence for Canines

If properly constructed, a fence provides your dog with a safe place to exercise and play. It also reduces the number of times you have to walk your dog. Although a fence does not replace a pleasant walk with your dog, it means you don't have to take your dog for a walk every time it wants to go out. In addition, a well-constructed fence often increases the value of your property. As well, a wooden fence provides privacy. Before constructing a fence to your specifications, ensure you have permission from all of the proper authorities.

Not wanting to use harmful chemicals or toxic preservatives, we opted for posts made of cedar (which contains a natural preservative). Three-foot holes were dug and the posts were cemented in. All the wood we used was

A fenced-in area provides your dog(s) with a safe place to exercise and play. Our fenced-in yard was ideal for the dogs because of its semi-rugged nature.

Photo: John Rutledge

purchased "rough cut" from a local sawmill. Besides being significantly cheaper, rough-cut wood absorbs stain well and does not require additional staining for years. (We did not stain the portion of the fence post below the ground.) In fact, once stained, the fence is virtually maintenance free. Stain provides some protection to the wood and comes in a variety of colours.

Besides the cedar posts, we used pine two-by-fours for the framing and pine one-by-sixes for the vertical fencing. Because of the jumping ability of some of our dogs, we built the fence six feet high. Also, because some of our dogs are diggers, a trench, approximately a foot wide and a foot deep, was dug between the fence posts. The trench was filled with rocks. The rocks were cemented together so our mischievous canines could not uproot the rocks and escape.

The yard we fenced is ideal for the dogs because of its semi-rugged nature. Besides the large crab apple tree, there are numerous, large bushes the dogs can play among and generally destroy at their own pleasure. As well, the yard features a birch tree and some transplanted white spruce.

While we do everything we can to make the fence "escape proof" we check on the dogs frequently to make sure they have not discovered a way of getting out of the yard.

Building an attractive and practical fence for your canine friends is considerable work, but a fence is convenient and, for some of us, a necessity. The benefits of a good fence are numerous. And isn't your "best friend" worth it?

Tasha enjoys the view from "her" picnic table, safe and sound in the fenced-in yard.

Photo: N. Glenn Perrett

Caring for
Your Dog

Photo: N. Glenn Perrett

15. Why Your Dog Should Be Neutered

Thousands of "unwanted" dogs are killed daily in North America. A small percentage of these animals may be destroyed because they are old, ill, injured or because they have a poor temperament. Unfortunately, the vast majority are killed for one simple reason: the supply of adoptable dogs is far greater than the demand of responsible people who are seeking to provide a pet with a good, caring home.

Who is to blame for this overpopulation? While no particular group is solely to blame, the major contributors to the problem are the irresponsible people who allow their dogs to breed indiscriminately. People who do not neuter their pets run the risk of them contributing to the overpopulation crisis. And if pets are allowed to run loose, the chance of unwanted litters increases significantly.

People who do not understand or care about the dog overpopulation crisis are irresponsible. They are oblivious to the neglect and suffering of animals.

Some ignorant or uncaring people actually allow their female dog to have litters of puppies. These people apparently think that as long as they find homes for all the puppies, everything is alright. They do not realize that for every good home one of their puppies takes, an animal waiting patiently in a shelter or pound will be killed due to a lack of a good home.

Other irresponsible people want to play "teacher" so that their children can learn from "the miracle of life." They feel it is educational for their children to watch the family pet having a litter. Do these people provide a complete lesson? Do they take their children to the local animal shelter or pound and show (and explain to them) the "tragedy of death"?

Often, well-meaning people who buy dogs from pet stores which have obtained their canine "inventory" from puppy mills (puppy farms) contribute, indirectly, to the dog

(Opposite) While the "puppy in the window" looks cute, chances are it came from a puppy mill where 'breeders' mass-produce puppies for pet stores.

overpopulation problem. Breeders who mass-produce puppies for pet stores are being supported by an unwary or uncaring public, who don't know about the disgusting conditions these puppies are "raised" in. Often forgotten, too, are the adult dogs used to produce the numerous litters. Many of these unfortunate creatures live in absolute squalor and are bred continually until their breeding days are over, at which time they are killed. The "puppy in the window" may look cute, but where did it come from? Chances are it originated from a puppy mill. Owners of puppy mills across North America produce hundreds of thousands of puppies annually. These breeders not only increase the dog overpopulation problem, but they also cause tremendous animal suffering and neglect in the process.

People who want to adopt a dog should do so at an animal shelter or pound or, if a purebred dog is desired, at a reputable breeder's facilities. Remember though, that while purebred dogs were once uncommon in animal shelters or pounds, this, tragically, is no longer the case.

Neutering

A neutered animal is a castrated male or a spayed female.

The mass destruction of "unwanted" dogs should be reason enough for people to have their dog neutered. Still not convinced? Read on.

Besides eliminating the possibility of your pet contributing to the escalating overpopulation problem, neutering your dog will eliminate or significantly decrease the risk of encountering some of the following medical problems:

Male Dog – testicular tumours (some of which are malignant); prostate problems; perineal hernias; certain skin and glandular growths dependent on male hormones.

Female Dog – ovarian tumours and uterine growths; potentially fatal uterine infection (pyometra); false pregnancies and mammary gland infections (mastitis); mammary tumours (many of which are malignant); death during whelping.

Here are some other benefits to neutering your dog: male dogs are less likely to roam and hence are less likely to be injured by cars, encounter rabid animals or fight with other animals; and problems associated with female dogs in heat will be eliminated.

The only dogs that should not be neutered include purebred canines used for breeding purposes and animals whose medical problems may increase their risk of not surviving an anaesthetic.

Some people believe that neutering their pet will change the animal's personality or that the animal will become fat after the operation. I have lived with thirteen dogs over the years, all of which were neutered. While Gandalf and Tasha were already neutered when we adopted them, the other dogs had to be neutered after they came to live with us. None of these dogs became fat or displayed any temperament or personality change after they were neutered. It is not true that neutered animals become fat. The animal's guardian is responsible to ensure this does not happen. Weight is primarily a function of food volume and exercise. Neutered pets usually require less food.

Then, there are those who say, "I wouldn't have it done to me so I won't have it done to my pet." This statement is ludicrous, as is the belief that female dogs should go through a heat or have a litter prior to being neutered. If you truly care for your dog, you will have it neutered, unless it is going to be bred for show purposes or your veterinarian recommends your pet not be neutered.

Having your dog neutered may save numerous unwanted animals from being destroyed. If these are not reasons enough, think of your pet: neutering your canine may save its life. Isn't your dog worth it?

(Opposite) Neutering a dog does not change the animal's personality. Prior to being spayed, Amorak was friendly, independent, extremely stubborn and occasionally mischievous — and she still is!

(Below) Purebred dogs are no longer uncommon in animal shelters and pounds. Tasha, a Siberian Husky, was acquired at an animal shelter — and she had already been spayed.

Photo: John Rutledge

16. Important Dog Care Items

Here is a list of items you will need for your dog.

Collar

A quality collar, which fits well, will enable you to take your pet for walks while on a leash, and it also provides a place to attach valuable identification tags. The collar should not only be properly fitted, it should also be durable, strong and easily cleaned. (For more about dog collars, see Chapter 17.)

Leash

Frequent walks are very important for a dog's physical and psychological well-being. A strong, four- to six-foot-long walking leash is adequate – especially for walks in urban or semi-urban environments.

An extended leash works well when exercising your dog in a park or countryside. Some extended leashes are just long ropes, with a handle on one end and a clip on the other that fastens to the dog's collar. Other leashes allow the dog to pull out several feet of line from the leash handle. This line is automatically re-coiled (within the handle) if the dog moves back towards the leash handle. The length of leash is controlled by pressing a button on the handle.

A leash allows a dog to exercise and allows the person walking the dog to have control. This is important for keeping the dog out of trouble while it runs around checking out its surroundings.

Bowls

A dog should have at least two bowls: one for its food and one for its water. If there are two or more dogs, then one water bowl is probably sufficient, unless there are many canine family members. Our eleven dogs manage quite well with two large water dishes (which are refilled several times daily).

While several dogs can share one or two water bowls, each dog should have its own food bowl, placed in its own section of the room or territory. This helps prevent fights over food. Lynn or I are always present when the dogs are fed to ensure that scuffles do not occur.

Stainless steel bowls are preferable because they are sanitary and easily cleaned. Do not use bowls made of glazed pottery. Some of these contain lead, which is poisonous.

Not all dogs need a crate, but these "dens" are beneficial with some canines in certain situations.

Photo: N. Glenn Perrett

Crate

Not everyone who lives with a dog provides a crate, but these "dens" for dogs are becoming increasingly popular. Puppies and mature dogs alike can be safely confined in a crate when their human companions are not able to ensure that the potentially mischievous canines will stay out of trouble.

Many adult dogs do not adjust to a crate if they've never had one, but puppies do, especially if they see the crate in a positive light and associate it with good times.

Feeding a dog in a crate and providing safe toys, blankets and other nice things will help ensure that the canine becomes comfortable with its own space. Do not put the dog in the crate as a form of punishment.

Our most-recent dogs have each been given a crate. The crate has provided them with a safe place to eat, a quiet place to sleep and, for those who seem prone to getting into trouble, a trouble-free place to stay when we cannot keep a watchful eye over them. Those dogs which have their own crates, along with some of those which do not, now voluntarily seek the refuge a crate provides when they want some quiet time to themselves. Crates can also provide a relatively secure and safe environment for your dog when it has to be transported.

Rawhide Bones

Rawhide bones provide dogs with a relatively safe item on which to chew. Chewing suitable products such as rawhide bones helps keep a dog's teeth strong and clean. Pressed rawhide bones are preferable to the knotted variety. With knotted ones, large pieces of rawhide can be swallowed, sometimes resulting in the animal choking. To be on the safe side, give your dog a rawhide bone only when you can be present to keep watch.

Toys

Like people, dogs enjoy a variety of toys. However, it is imperative that a dog's toys be safe. If you are not sure what toys are trouble-free, check with your veterinarian or qualified employees of pet supply stores to learn what is appropriate. In general, soft plastic toys, which are easily chewed apart, and "squeaky" toys, where the squeaker is easily removed, should be avoided. As well, if your dog has a ball, ensure that the ball is large enough so it can't be swallowed.

Grooming Equipment

Some dogs require very little in the way of grooming; others need considerable attention. People who can afford a professional dog groomer require less equipment than those of us who tend to all of our pets' grooming needs ourselves.

Lynn and I groom all of our dogs. We do this for several reasons: the time involved with transporting dogs back and forth to the groomers; the money that's saved; and the fact that it's relatively easy to do and provides some important one-on-one interaction with each of our dogs. While Lynn and I may not do as "professional" a job, it is a quick and relatively stress-free procedure for the dogs (and ourselves).

Because our dogs' hair is as unique and different as each of our dogs, we require an assortment of grooming equipment. We have three different types of brushes. A soft brush is used regularly on our dogs whose coats are short, relatively clean and are not shedding. When our short-haired dogs are shedding, we use a brush consisting of long, flexible bristles. We also use this brush on our long-haired dogs from time to time. With our Huskies, who have a dense undercoat, we use a wire brush – especially when they are shedding.

Because Brandy, our Wirehaired Fox Terrier, had a coat that required trimming every few months, we purchased a set of electric trimmers. These clippers, along with a couple of blades, which trim the hair coat to different lengths, allowed us to cut Brandy's coat to an appropriate length (depending on the season). While the outcome was never in line to win grooming awards, it did allow us to maintain Brandy's beautiful, yet at times rather difficult, coat in good order. These same clippers are also used on Winston, our Terrier cross.

Bathing

Besides brushing your pet's hair coat, you will also need to bathe your canine companion from time to time – unless you can afford to pay someone else to do it. Remember though, that dogs are supposed to smell like dogs. Bathe your dogs as often as is necessary but do not overdo it. Our dogs are bathed once a year, unless they have gotten some foreign material in their hair coat that cannot be brushed out. Use a mild shampoo, such as a baby shampoo, to bathe your dog.

There are times when a dog should not be bathed: sick dogs, young puppies, bitches in whelp and dogs that have recently been operated on. If you are unsure as to whether your dog should be bathed, consult your veterinarian.

Nail Trimming

Unless your veterinarian or groomer trims your dog's nails, it will be up to you to keep them at an appropriate length. Human nail clippers can be used on puppies, but clip only the very tip of the nail. For mature dogs you will need commercially available nail clippers. Again, only remove a small portion of the nail regularly, as opposed to removing a larger amount on an infrequent basis. Have the appropriate materials on hand in case a nail is clipped too short and bleeds. There are products available to treat bleeding nails. Dogs that are frequently walked on pavement may not require regular nail trimming, but you should occasionally inspect the nails to be sure.

Emergency Medical Kit

An emergency medical kit for your dog is a good idea. Bandages and hydrogen peroxide may be used to temporarily treat small lacerations or minor abscesses. Products such as Kaopectate may be used to treat a mild bout of diarrhea. Ask your veterinarian what items you should stock and how they should be used, in case an emergency situation arises.

Finally, an emergency kit doesn't replace a veterinarian. Treating minor scrapes yourself is fine. As well, it may be necessary to provide some preliminary care for your dog before taking it to a veterinarian. (If your dog is seriously cut, you might need to stop, or significantly reduce, the bleeding by applying pressure to the wound before rushing the injured animal to a veterinarian.) However, too often,

well-meaning people take their dog to a veterinarian only after attempting to treat the dog themselves, and after proper treatment is beyond hope. This is tragic. In many instances, the dog could have been successfully treated if it had received proper care sooner.

17. Effective Identification and Quality Collars

For a responsible guardian, there are few feelings worse than when a beloved canine goes missing. When one of my dogs escapes the premises, I experience panic, followed immediately by a terrible feeling in my chest. Anxiety escalates as I give chase to my curious canine, who is too interested in the sights and sounds to heed my feeble warnings. If I happen to lose sight of my dog, the feelings of terror increase even more. At times like these, I wish my dogs were better trained.

Although Lynn and I have always managed to retrieve our canines shortly after their escaping (this has occurred only a few times), the feeling that they will become lost, a road casualty or meet some other terrible fate is truly dreadful. I cannot imagine enduring that agony for days. Some people never see their pet again. It must be extremely painful wondering what became of a lost, cherished pet.

Eliminating the chances of your dog becoming lost is virtually impossible. However, there are ways of significantly increasing the chances of a quick and safe return of your canine if it happens to go missing.

Remaining calm while implementing an effective "plan of attack" is very important. Besides "pounding the pavement," posting signs with your pet's picture and relevant information increases the chances of a successful reunion. If you have not located your dog within a few hours, you

(Opposite) Teddy was a fortunate stray who found a home the day he wandered into our yard. He had no identification or even a collar. After unsuccessfully attempting to locate his keeper(s), we welcomed the friendly German Shepherd cross into our family.

should contact all the humane societies, pounds and veterinary clinics in your area, as well as checking other appropriate spots. These places should be contacted on a regular basis; once a day is not unreasonable.

Identification

A methodical search for a lost or stray animal is of utmost importance. But having the foresight to equip your pet with identification that can be easily traced significantly improves the chances of a safe return. Unfortunately, most guardians do not equip their pet with identification. Those that do, often use identification which is not easily traced.

Identification methods include a dog licence, a personalized pet identification tag, or microchips. Whatever form is used, it should be safe for your dog and easy to notice and to use for tracing.

Tattoos, another means of identification, have been around for some time, especially for purebred dogs. But tattoos are often hidden or are difficult to read, and many employees in animal shelters, pounds and veterinary clinics do not take the time to look for tattoos on stray dogs. Even when tattoo combinations are found, there is still the process of tracing the guardian, which can usually only be done during business hours.

Similarly, rabies tags and dog licences are not effective forms of pet identification. Dog licences can be traced but, again, only during office hours. What happens if someone finds a stray or lost dog at 6 p.m. on a Friday? Will the dog be looked after until its guardian can be contacted on Monday? Not likely.

As well, rabies tags can only be traced during the working hours of the veterinary clinic which issued the tag. I once found an overheated, tired, disoriented, old dog limping around in the middle of a large city on a very hot Saturday afternoon.

Lynn and I took the dog to our house, an hour north of the city, and set to work trying to find the dog's guardian(s). We posted numerous signs in the surrounding neighbourhoods where we found the little dog. We also contacted the humane society in the city and the animal shelters, pounds and veterinary clinics in the immediate area as well as in the surrounding regions.

The only tag on the dog's collar was an outdated rabies tag. No name of a veterinary clinic was on the tag – only the company that issued the tag. I called the company on Monday morning and was able to get the name of the veterinary clinic that issued the tag. Unfortunately the tag was issued during a special rabies clinic and the veterinary staff had not bothered to keep records.

So, while rabies tags are usually a form of identification, occasionally they are not. In this case the tag did nothing more than provide a false sense of security. The tag could not be traced.

The dog and its guardian were eventually re-united with the help of the humane society. The dog had escaped from its yard, several blocks away, after someone failed to close the gate.

Few people will take on the responsibility of caring for a "stray" pet until its home can be found via a licence or rabies tag. Those that do rarely put themselves out very much. People who cannot trace the pet's guardian immediately, opt to let the animal continue wandering, assuring themselves that the animal will go home. Unfortunately, many of these pets are lost. Wandering is a dangerous pastime for dogs; the chance of it becoming a road casualty or meeting another terrible fate is considerable.

While rabies and licence tags may be helpful in returning lost pets, a more effective way is a personalized identification tag, with at least your phone number – including the area code on it. Your address engraved on the tag is also a good idea.

Identification tags should be regularly checked to ensure they are firmly affixed to the collar. When you do, make sure the information is still easy to read. Identification tags are invaluable for re-uniting lost pets with their families. With the number on the tag, the animal's human guardian can be contacted immediately – day or night.

Modern technology has recently made a contribution to pet identification. Microchips and scanners are becoming more common in identifying lost or stray pets. Pets "in-jected" with a microchip can be traced to their homes with the help of a scanner, a scanner operator and a computer line.

Many veterinary clinics, animal control agencies and humane societies are acquiring these devices for identifying pets. Microchip identification has numerous benefits, including the fact that it is always with your pet. However, many pounds, veterinary clinics and humane societies have not implemented this program. Another problem is that lost pets cannot be returned immediately to their families. Pets with microchips must have the scanner passed over them before the computer line can be used to collect information. Those wearing tags with a phone number are only a call away from being re-united with their keepers.

While the local clinic or animal control may have the microchip/scanner program, chances are they will not respond to a "routine" call concerning a stray pet when the office is closed.

If this form of identification is used, check with the distributor or supplier as to the exact services provided and the costs involved.

Collars

Good identification is very important for dogs, but so are quality collars. Choke chains are not appropriate for casual use. Dogs can die if their choke chain becomes caught on an object or somehow becomes tightened around the dog's neck. Dogs should only wear choke chains during training sessions. But use identification tags on the training collar as well; dogs can "escape" while being trained!

Our dogs wear adjustable collars made from soft, strong nylon. The collars come in a variety of colours and are even

(Opposite) Winston was noticed on a highway. A piece of rope was dangling from his collar. The frightened and tired stray dog evaded our attempts to catch him for two days. He was finally enticed into our care with some food several kilometres from where we first noticed him. After all attempts to locate his guardian(s) failed (there was no identification on the collar), we adopted the spirited Terrier.

available with a reflective strip. These collars feature a two-inch, limited-slip design, which allows the collar to loosen slightly when it is not being pulled. Because the collar normally lays loose around the dog's neck, wear and tear to the dog's coat is minimized. When pulled, the collar tightens to hold the dog securely. These collars, if properly adjusted, do not choke the dog when pulled, but rather tighten sufficiently so the collar cannot be pulled over the dog's head. A collar should not be so loose that it can be pulled over your dog's head, but it should be loose enough that you can fit two fingers between the collar and the dog's neck.

Durable, nylon, embroidered pet collars are becoming more and more popular. Nylon collars with your full phone number embroidered on them are not only attractive and practical (most dogs require a collar anyway), but as with personalized identification tags they allow people finding your pet to phone you immediately. While many people will not "put themselves out" finding a stray or lost pet's guardian, many will take the time to phone the number on a pet's collar or tag. Some people also opt to have their dog's name embroidered on the collar, along with their telephone number. If there is not enough room for both the pet's name and full telephone number, it is more important to include the area code.

Personalized pet collars need to be replaced or changed whenever the owner's phone number changes. As well, the thread used for the numbers and letters can become worn and faded. By carefully contrasting the colour of thread for the embroidery with the colour of the collar, the result is an attractive collar which can be easily read.

While any identification is helpful, some methods are better than others. Personalized identification tags and collars, are preferable. However, microchip identification sounds interesting, certainly worth discussing with your veterinarian.

For people who are extremely cautious, the logical approach might be to equip their dog with both a microchip and an embroidered, personalized collar or identification tag. The choice is yours. But don't forget to do it.

18. Reducing the Chances of Your Canine Becoming Lost

Every year thousands of canines go missing. Many of these pets have easily escaped their human guardians; others have been more opportunistic or devious in gaining access to the "outside" (and dangerous) world. While many dogs are simply exploring the surrounding area and will return – provided they do not get hit by a car or meet a similarly nasty fate – others will become lost. There are few sadder sights than a lost dog desperately trying to find its way back home.

No matter how careful you are, if you have a canine family member, there is a good chance that at some time you will be looking for a lost dog. On those few occasions when one of our dogs has left our company without our permission, we have either been fortunate enough to retrieve it quickly, or the animal has thankfully returned after a short time of exploring.

Many dogs are not nearly as fortunate. Numerous pets tragically end up as "road kills." Some die of starvation or succumb to the elements. Some meet other undesirable fates. A few lost dogs are lucky to be picked up by animal control, returned to their human guardians, or adopted. Unfortunately, because there are so many more dogs than there are good homes for them, a staggering number of friendly canines are destroyed.

Reducing the chances of your four-legged family member from becoming lost means using common sense.

It may sound obvious, but if you always know where your pet is, it will not be lost. Ensuring that your dog is not allowed off of your property unattended is a good start. Many dogs are allowed unintentional "freedom" when someone carelessly opens a door, allowing a canine access to the out-of-doors, or opens a gate to a fenced-in yard. Children are often guilty of this. But so, too, are people who are not aware that you have a dog and that the animal is not allowed outside without a leash (and with someone holding the leash) or without human supervision. These people often include friends or people who may have access to your home, such as repairmen, while you are out.

Lynn and I virtually eliminate the possibility of our dogs leaving our property without us. We keep locks on the gates to our fenced-in yard. We keep our doors locked, even when we are at home. And we only allow people in our house when we are at home. The mudrooms adjacent to our three exterior doors are also effective. We have a "house rule" that the mudroom door to the outside cannot be opened until the door into the house is securely closed.

If your dog goes missing, you will increase your chances of getting your dog returned if you have a clear, colour (preferably), up-to-date photograph of your pet. Copies of this photograph can be placed, along with a written description of your pet and how you can be contacted, at appropriate locations (see Chapter 19). If colour photographs are not available, black-and-white photographs (or photocopies of a photograph) of your dog with description and your telephone number, will help alert people to the fact that your dog is missing.

Pets sometimes become lost when their human guardians go to an area unfamiliar to the animal. In these situations it is very important that the animal has good identification (see Chapter 17). The animal can easily become disoriented in strange surroundings. Knowing where your pet is is very important when frequenting places unfamiliar to your dog.

Effective identification and always knowing where your pet is will go a long way to reducing the chances of your dog becoming lost. Using common sense and carefully thinking about ways to keep your dog safe and happy can help avert a potentially tragic situation.

19. Looking for a Lost Dog

It is important to remain as calm as possible and to set a "plan of attack" in motion to find the lost pet quickly.

Check every part of the house and yard. Dogs can hide in the darndest places. Call your pet by name and listen. Maybe it cannot move, but it may bark or whimper or howl.

Next, search the immediate area around your property and ask everyone if they have seen your dog. Show a colour photograph of your pet and give people your name and phone number in case they happen to see your pet.

If, after a few hours, you have not located your dog, contact all the humane societies, veterinary clinics, animal shelters and pounds in your area. Give a full description of your pet including any distinguishing features such as breed, size, sex, colouring, scars, tatoos or limps. Again, have the photograph so you can provide every little detail of your pet's appearance. Leave your home and work phone numbers. Ensure that the phone is not "tied up" in case someone is trying to call. Often people call because they have just seen your pet go by. You have to respond to these calls quickly.

Since dogs can cover a large territory quickly, also call the pounds, shelters and veterinary clinics beyond your immediate area. Perhaps your pet has travelled farther and faster than you thought. Possibly someone picked up your pet as a stray and took it to a shelter or pound farther away than the "local" animal shelter. At each shelter, pound and veterinary clinic, ask for additional places you should be notifying. As well, contact radio stations that broadcast missing pet announcements.

Distributing signs describing your missing pet is important. Print the word "lost" in big, bold letters at the top of the sign. "Reward" is an even better word, if you are offering one. It will attract attention – especially among children, who are often the most help in finding lost pets.

Other important information for the sign includes when and where the pet was lost, a description of the pet including age and markings, a description of the collar and any identification tags it was wearing. Make sure your name, address and phone number(s) are on the sign. A good photograph of your dog on the sign, especially if it is in colour, is best. Make copies of a photo or, if this is not possible, colour photocopies. These should provide a good visual description of your dog. If this is not possible, put a photo of your dog on one sign and have several photocopies made. Signs using bright-coloured paper, such as yellow, will attract people's attention.

Good locations for these signs are street posts, post offices, convenience/grocery stores, laundromats, and other frequently visited areas. Where applicable, get permission from the store owner, manager or employee to post your signs. Once your pet is found, make sure these signs are removed.

Signs should also be distributed at veterinary clinics, pounds and animal shelters. It often pays to leave a photograph, preferably in colour, of your pet at these places. Since animal shelters and pounds are usually very busy, visit these places every couple of days. Ask what the minimum time is that each pound or animal shelter holds an animal. (Many places only hold animals for an extremely short period.)

Make a daily routine of contacting shelters, pounds and veterinary clinics. Check the yellow pages of your phone book for the veterinary clinics in your area. Putting "lost" ads in newspapers and checking the "found" ads is also important.

Try to think of "extra" things you can do to help retrieve your lost dog. Politely asking the assistance of people who are frequently out in the region (and bordering regions) in which your dog went missing is often helpful. Some of these people include postal workers, school bus drivers, roads department employees, as well as those people who collect your garbage and recyclables, to name but a few. Give them your name, address and phone number, along with a description of your dog. (Give them one of your signs.) The more people you enlist to help, the better. Again, offering a reward often helps. The reward does not have to break your budget. However, offering a reward, either during a conversation or in an advertisement, draws added attention to your situation.

Conducting an organized and efficient search for a lost pet is important, but having a pet identification tag with your phone number attached to your dog's collar is the most valuable step you can take now, to avoid a crisis.

Ensure that your pet always has adequate identification. Keep a colour photograph of your dog. Know where your pet is, at all times. But, if your pet goes missing, have an action plan.

20. Caring for a Physically Challenged Dog

A few years ago Lynn and I were presented with the opportunity of adopting a phycially challenged dog. While the last thing we needed was another canine, the fact that the dog was a young, female puppy meant she would probably get along with our other dogs and even be tolerated by Winston, our Terrier cross.

This particular dog was one of several puppies, and while the others were healthy, this puppy had serious problems with her legs, so serious, in fact, that when we first saw the puppy she had never stood up – and she was three months of age! The puppy, whom we named Samantha, got around by wriggling slowly.

The staff at the veterinary clinic, who did not want to destroy the little dog, had improved her condition considerably through physiotherapy. They hoped she would progress enough to lead a "semi-normal" life.

When Lynn first set eyes on the tiny puppy (she weighed only five pounds), I knew we would not be leaving without adopting the little dog. Part of our rationale for adopting yet another canine was: "How much trouble could a dog be if it could not walk?" Did we have a lot to learn! Actually, before we left for home that day, Samantha stood up for the first time for a treat from our veterinarian. This was a good sign.

We left Samantha at the clinic for another month for more physiotherapy, as well as treatment for an infection she had developed. This gave us time to prepare for Samantha's arrival. We bought her a couple of small dishes and prepared her crate. As well, a friend of ours made a special bed that Samantha could easily wriggle into, as well as a pillow and dog sweater. This dog was spoiled and we did not even have her yet!

When Lynn and I took Samantha home a month later, she had progressed to the point where she could "walk" a little. We have had Samantha for a few years now. Her hind legs are still fragile and somewhat deformed, but they are getting stronger, and she can walk several hundred yards at a time. While this walking is somewhat laboured, she gets around quite well and continues to improve. She can even run short distances and takes pleasure chasing the larger dogs, nipping at their hind legs. She can even jump up on the couch, although it may take a few attempts!

While Samantha has improved considerably, we would have adopted her even if there was no chance of her walking. Some people may think it is cruel to keep a physically challenged pet. It is not cruel if the animal is happy or content.

Prolonging the animal's life is usually not a good idea if the animal is suffering considerably and there is no chance of the suffering being eliminated or reduced. Even when Samantha could not stand up, much less walk, she was one of the happiest puppies I have seen. Something as simple as a rawhide bone or picking her up made this happy puppy ecstatic.

Physically challenged pets are usually very adoptable. I have seen dogs and cats get along efficiently on three legs. Although some people would not adopt these pets for a variety of "reasons," I believe they should be given every opportunity for full and happy lives.

A special bond has existed between Lynn and Samantha since Lynn first set eyes on the tiny, physically challenged puppy.

Photo: John Rutledge

21. Visiting Your Pet in the Hospital

Lynn and I went through the very difficult situation of having Brandy, our Wirehaired Fox Terrier "put to sleep." Brandy had developed a malignant tumour, which stretched across the width of her abdomen and was pushing on her bowels. She also had numerous smaller tumours growing inside her.

Our veterinarian, Dr. Kim St. John, who is also our cousin, informed us that while Brandy was not yet suffering, she was feeling some discomfort. His prognosis was poor; Brandy had only a few days to live. Because she was very weak, was not eating and was uncomfortable, Lynn and I realized that euthanasia was the only humane solution (see Chapter 30).

Three days after losing Brandy, Lynn and I went through another emotional experience: Amorak, our Siberian Husky, began getting stiff in her hind legs and was panting excessively. She looked uncomfortable.

Beginning to panic, especially after having just lost Brandy, we phoned Dr. St. John. Arrangements were made for Lynn to take the next day off work to drive Amorak to see Dr. St. John, who was located approximately one hundred miles away.

Although we didn't think Amorak's condition was serious, we wanted to be sure. Was I in for a shock. She did not return home with Lynn that evening. Amorak's stiffness worsened to the point where she was dragging her hind legs. She also had to be put on intravenous and injected with antibiotics and cortisone to cover a large number of possible causes.

Amorak's condition worsened. She experienced a lack of skin sensation over her croup and had two minor convulsions. She was kept on intravenous and given anticonvulsants. Dr. St. John contacted a veterinary neurologist in a nearby city to ensure that his treatment for Amorak was all that could be done – which it was. It was confirmed that Amorak had encephalitis.

Rabies is one form of this disease, so it was not ruled out. I was sure that Amorak did not have rabies; she had been confined to our property whenever she was let out and had been watched carefully. However, the possibility made an extremely upsetting situation even more terrifying.

Amorak's condition continued to deteriorate. Ascending paralysis immobilized her front and back legs. Even her eyes were affected. At this stage Dr. St. John was not optimistic.

Due to the seriousness of Amorak's condition, Lynn and I began to wonder if we should visit Amorak. Having seen how emotional Lynn and I were with Brandy, Dr. St. John felt we would not do ourselves any good to see Amorak in such a terrible state. After all, our five-year-old dog was paralyzed; even her eyes were not functioning properly.

While Lynn and I had been upset with losing Brandy, there was some comfort in knowing she had had a full,

Photo: Norman W. Perrett

56

happy life. It was quite a different situation with Amorak, who was only five, had been so full of life, and was dying. I began to feel sorry for myself and to convince myself that going to see Amorak was not a good idea. After all, what could we do? Would Amorak even recognize us?

Later, one of my calls to Dr. St. John was taken by his wife, Shelley, who asked if we would be coming down to see Amorak. I told Shelley what Dr. St. John had told us, and my apprehension was probably obvious. However, Shelley, not one for "beating around the bush," made a statement I will not soon forget: "If it were my dog I would be there." That made sense. After all, what did we have to lose by going? If Amorak did not recognize us, she would be no worse off. However, if she was aware of our presence it might im-

The author, holding Brandy, and his Nana holding Amorak who was only six weeks old.

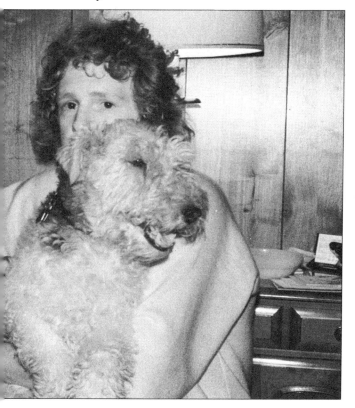

prove her condition or, at the very least, give her comfort. Shelley's comment made me stop feeling sorry for myself and start trying to help Amorak.

The next afternoon, after work, Lynn and I drove to the veterinary clinic, and it was with an uneasy feeling that we approached Amorak's cage. When we bent down and looked into Amorak's eyes and spoke to her, Amorak whined. This sign reassured me. She could not move but she knew we were there and responded to our presence. While I winced at Amorak's whine, it was reassuring to know she acknowledged our presence and seemed to be telling us that she was not giving up. An examination conducted by Dr. St. John showed that there was a little feeling in Amorak's legs.

Lynn and I sat and talked with her. We also patted and brushed her. We hoped that by spending time with and grooming Amorak we would comfort and stimulate her, thereby increasing her chances for a recovery. Amorak acknowledged us by whining occasionally. Spending time with Amorak seemed to reassure us as well as Amorak.

After dinner, we returned to the veterinary clinic. While Amorak had little feeling in her legs, her ears twitched and her eyes were more responsive. In fact, with a little help, she was able to sit up. We drove home late that night.

After work the next day, Lynn and I again drove to visit with Amorak. The specialist who was kept informed of her condition was still not reassuring. Although Amorak was a little weaker, her appetite had improved and she was more alert, and she recognized us. Lynn and I made the trek home late that evening.

The next day (Friday) we were extremely tired and wanted to rest before visiting Amorak on the weekend. We kept in touch with the clinic by phone and were told that Amorak tried to sit up and, when supported, tried to use three legs to walk.

On Saturday morning Amorak looked alert, could sit up and could walk if her hind end was supported. She was making excellent progress!

After spending part of the afternoon at the St. Johns' we all went to see Amorak that evening. She looked better than she had earlier in the day and her hind legs were coming around. Lynn and I stayed over at the St. Johns' that night.

On Sunday, Amorak was standing and waiting for us. She knocked the cage door open when the bolt was unfastened, and was even able to go for a short walk unassisted. When we left later that day, we felt much better. While Amorak had not made a full recovery, she had improved tremendously.

We kept in touch with the clinic by telephone and on Tuesday were told that we could pick up Amorak. Tuesday night, after work, Lynn and I drove to the clinic and brought Amorak home.

It had been thirteen days since Brandy had been put to sleep. We were beginning to think of the veterinary clinic as our "home away from home." What made the two weeks bearable (during which we had to say farewell to Brandy and had almost lost Amorak) was all the support we had from both family and friends – and the staff at the clinic. They knew how Lynn and I were hurting because of Brandy and seemed to rally behind Amorak. While the staff gives all pets excellent care, they seemed to give Amorak special attention.

While we can't "prove" our visits helped Amorak get better, I am convinced they did. Dr. St. John also believes our visits aided Amorak's speedy recovery.

Visiting an injured or sick pet in the hospital, however, is not always preferable. In most instances, a pet recuperating from an operation or a broken bone will only get excited and its condition could worsen.

Amorak, however, must have been totally confused as to why she could no longer move and why she was experiencing convulsions. Our presence likely comforted Amorak; she was aware that we had not abandoned her. I think our presence reassured Amorak, which, in turn, gave her the hope and strength she needed to get well again. Keeping Amorak's spirit up was likely important in her recovery.

The best time for visits is when the clinic is relatively quiet and the client will not be in the way of the day-to-day activities. People who believe that visiting their sick or injured animal in the veterinary hospital may be beneficial should ask their veterinarian for permission, and arrange a convenient visiting schedule.

It has been approximately six years since Amorak had encephalitis. She made a complete recovery. Regular visits to the hospital, combined with the special care she received from the veterinary staff, not to mention Amorak's own amazing recuperative powers were all instrumental in her getting well.

It has been approximately six years since Amorak had encephalitis. She made a complete recovery.

Protecting Your Dog

22. Vaccinating is a Must

Dogs, like humans, require protection against disease. To eliminate or significantly reduce your pet's exposure to disease, avoid places that have a high likelihood of being contaminated. This is especially true for young dogs that have not been fully inoculated. Places that have a higher risk of being contaminated include areas frequented by dogs, such as parks and kennels.

It is also vital to have your dog vaccinated against the appropriate diseases. Discuss with your veterinarian what your dog should be vaccinated for and how often, and set up a vaccination/examination schedule. Keep a file, at home, with all of the animal's records (medical and other).

Not only does vaccinating your dog offer your pet protection, but it also offers you some protection from diseases your pet could get and transmit to you, such as rabies.

Another important reason for vaccinations is that it is much easier, not to mention less expensive, to prevent disease than it is to treat the disease. And the sick dog may die!

A vaccine is composed of a disease agent, which has been altered so that the animal builds an immunity to that disease. Some of the vaccines given to dogs can protect them from rabies, parvovirus, distemper, infectious canine hepatitis, canine adenovirus, canine parainfluenza, canine bordetellosis and corona virus. Some vaccines contain a single agent; others contain a combination of agents.

Having your canine vaccinated as often as your dog's doctor feels it is necessary is a vital part of properly raising your "best friend." There is no reason to expose your dog to disease needlessly when there are effective and safe vaccines available.

(Opposite) Young puppies are extremely susceptible to canine parvovirus. Vaccinating your dog against this potentially deadly virus will reduce the chances of your pet contracting "parvo." Remember to have your dog vaccinated as often as your veterinarian recommends.

Canine Parvovirus

I am illustrating the need for vaccinations by describing just one of the diseases that can attack your canine friend.

Canine parvovirus is a serious virus. Young puppies are extremely susceptible to this virus, although dogs of all ages can be infected.

Parvovirus is readily transmitted from dog to dog, from people to dogs (petting infected animals), or directly to dogs from contaminated areas. Parvovirus is distributed via the feces of infected dogs.

Common signs that a dog has become infected include vomiting, diarrhea, dehydration, lethargy, depression and anorexia. As well, vomit and stools may contain blood and the animal may have an elevated body temperature.

Dogs affected by this virus either die rather quickly or recover slowly. The earlier the infected animal is treated the better the prognosis will be.

While parvovirus can be deadly, you can significantly reduce the chance of your dog getting "parvo." When you acquire your canine family member, have it examined by your veterinarian. Remember to have your dog vaccinated as often as your veterinarian recommends.

Besides keeping your dog up-to-date with its vaccinations, you can take other precautions to help guard your canine from this serious virus. For example, avoid areas frequented by numerous dogs, such as dog kennels, dog shows and parks. This is particularly important for young dogs, especially if they have not been inoculated against parvovirus or have only received one parvovirus vaccination. It is a fine line to follow to both socialize a puppy and protect it from health risks such as parvovirus.

Another way to help protect your dog from health risks such as parvovirus is to keep your pet's environment clean. And keep a watchful eye on your "best friend." If it appears lethargic, has diarrhea, vomits, or exhibits any of the other symptoms associated with parvovirus, do not take these signs lightly. Have your dog examined by a veterinarian.

If you follow these precautions and use common sense, you will be doing your part to protect your canine family member from this potentially deadly virus.

23. Protecting Your Dog from Poisons and other Hazards

The problem of poisons exists throughout the year. However, the risk of your dog being exposed to harmful chemicals increases significantly in the spring and summer. During these seasons, people use potentially harmful chemicals – spraying and fertilizing their lawns, shrubs and trees; painting their houses; and using their barbecues. Often the problem is how the product is stored, as opposed to how the product is actually used. Another hazard is plants that contain toxic substances.

Causes and Preventions

A common group of herbicides harmful to animals is phenoxy herbicides, which are often used as weed killers. Dogs are particularly sensitive to this group. Often, problems associated with these herbicides happen while they are in storage, in their concentrated form.

Kerosene and other petroleum distillates comprise another group that are very harmful to animals. Included in this group are such products as charcoal lighting fluid, ether, naphtha, paint thinner, fuel and lubricating oils, lacquer thinner, and rubber solvents. Fuel, solvents and cleaning agents are also common ingredients in garden sprays and insecticides. These petroleum distillates may cause weakness, lack of coordination, vomiting, diarrhea, rapid breathing and shock.

Metaldehyde, which is used as snail and slug bait, is a potentially fatal substance. If you use metaldehyde baits, place them where your pet cannot get any access.

Organophosphates and carbamates are two large groups of insecticides or parasiticides. Often, animals have convulsions if they are exposed to these substances.

Phenol, commonly used as a wood preservative or as a disinfectant, can also be very harmful to animals. Creosote, pine tar, carbolic acid and lysol are common products containing phenol.

Another hazard (to animals in general and children) is the misuse of rat poisons. Some commonly used rat poisons are arsenic, Warfarin, Red Squill and ANTU. The best solution when using rat poison is to ensure that animals, other than rats, cannot get near the poison. Placement of the poison is very important. To avoid secondary poisoning, which can often prove fatal for pets, all rats (and other animals) that have died as a result of the rat poison should be immediately disposed of safely. Better still, do not use rat poison. If you have a rat problem, solve it in a humane, non-toxic manner.

In spring, people store their antifreeze, which contains ethylene glycol – also present in brake fluid and other substances. Lock these substances in a storage cabinet or place them well out of the reach of dogs and other animals. They are often attracted to this toxic substance because of its sweet taste. Common signs that an animal has ingested ethylene glycol are vomiting and weakness. Once ingested, ethylene glycol causes severe and often irreparable damage to the kidneys. Any antifreeze or brake fluid (or any other substance containing ethylene glycol) that is spilt should be immediately and thoroughly cleaned up.

If you use lawn and garden sprays, know what chemicals are contained in the spray, and know how these chemicals can affect your pet. Take the necessary precautions to avoid accidental poisonings. If potentially harmful chemicals have been used, then post a sign alerting people to these chemicals at the affected area.

A better alternative to pesticides and herbicides is not to use these substances on your lawn and garden. What is wrong with the odd weed? Dumping chemicals on your lawns and gardens is costly, harms the environment, and may even harm your pet or yourself!

Treatment

If your dog is poisoned, act responsibly and quickly. The phone number of your veterinarian and the poison control centre should be close at hand. Call your veterinarian for advice. If you are sure of the poisoning substance, contact the poison control centre for advice, if the animal is not showing any adverse symptoms. However, if illness or abnormal behaviour is becoming apparent, contact a veterinarian immediately. If possible, have the name of the toxic substance, as well as a rough idea of the amount ingested, inhaled or absorbed and the time the poisoning occurred.

In some instances it may be necessary to induce vomiting. If so, force-feed your pet enough hydrogen peroxide to make it vomit. If this treatment is not productive, repeat in five minutes and seek professional advice. Don't induce vomiting if the dog has swallowed bleach, strong acids, or strongly alkaline substances. These materials burn on their way down, and will burn on their way up.

If a poison has been absorbed through the skin, bathe and rinse the animal, using a mild dish detergent. Contact your veterinarian for instructions as to whether to bathe the animal first or to have the pet examined immediately. This will depend on the presence or absence of adverse signs. If bathing the animal is suggested, gloves should be worn if the substance is highly toxic. Check the label on the container.

Since the ingestion of toxic substances can cause convulsions, it is important to wrap the animal in a blanket or other heavy material so it cannot harm itself while thrashing around. Be extremely careful when working around the head of a convulsing animal: they are unaware of what is going on and can cause serious bite wounds. Bring the container of the suspected poison to the veterinary hospital along with the animal. There are antidotes for certain poisons, and you should try to discover what the animal has ingested, inhaled or absorbed.

When transporting the animal, ensure that it is wrapped, if it appears cool or cold, as if in shock. A hot-water bottle can be used as well. Make sure there is a sheet or blanket between the animal and the hot-water bottle as direct contact can burn the animal's skin.

If your pet has been poisoned, it may be necessary to leave the animal in the hospital for a few days for appropriate medical treatment, which often includes intravenous fluids, antibiotics and anticonvulsants.

Other Preventative Measures

Poisoning can often be avoided by being careful and using common sense. In many cases, poisoning results not from how a product is used but from improper storage. If harmful substances are locked away or placed on high shelves, out of the reach of animals, most cases of poisoning can be avoided.

Another way to poison prevention is to reduce the toxic substances you use. There are alternatives. For example, instead of using metaldehyde for snail and slug control, try a common non-toxic approach – beer. Set out jar lids or saucers full of beer. Slugs and snails will be attracted to the fermented liquid. Usually, the slugs and snails will literally "drown in their own drink."

There are viable and safe alternatives to chemical sprays for trees as well. In fact, there are numerous books that describe not only safe and humane ways to solving problems involving "nuisance" wildlife but also "natural" insect and disease control methods in gardening, which do not involve dangerous and hazardous substances.

Although plants play an important role in our lives, they can bring an element of danger – especially to family pets. According to the Humane Society of the United States, "More than 700 plants have been identified as producing physiologically active or toxic substances in sufficient amounts to cause harmful effects in animals."

Poisonous plants can cause five general but different physiological reactions. Toxic substances from plants have been classified as blood poisons, muscular poisons, neuromuscular poisons, neurological poisons and irritants.

Often, common plants that we think of as being harmless are, in fact, poisonous. Two that fall into this category are buttercups and daffodils. The entire buttercup plant is toxic, but especially the leaves. The toxic part of daffodil plants is the bulb. Knowing the poisonous plants found on your property as well as those harmful plants located in your home, and not allowing animals access to these, will also reduce the possibility of accidental poisonings. (A longer list can be found in Appendix A.)

For information about any toxic substance, contact the poison control centre in your area.

Find the telephone number of the poison control centre in your area and make sure it is easily accessible. (The phone numbers of these centres do change occasionally. Don't wait for an emergency to find that the poison control centre phone number has changed.) As well, have your veterinarian's phone number and the emergency "after hours" phone number readily available.

Do all this and you will be off to a good start in poison proofing your home and helping to ensure that your "best friend" remains healthy.

24. Fleas!

Most people who own a dog experience problems with the dreaded flea, at one time or another. Even those who carefully try to avoid the nuisance flea often find themselves faced with the difficult task of ridding their pet and premises of the wingless, bloodsucking insects.

Fleas are not usually acquired from outdoor areas such as parks and gardens, but rather from places that have carrier animals – kennels, pounds, animal shelters and veterinary clinics.

Fleas are wingless, dark-brown insects capable of jumping great distances. They obtain their nourishment by sucking the blood of warm-blooded animals. Fleas are carriers of tapeworm cysts and can also cause allergic dermatitis.

Adult fleas are visible to the human eye. If an animal has fleas, then the flea feces (partially digested blood) will likely be in your pet's coat. A good way to see if your dog has fleas is to moisten a piece of plain, white tissue paper and hold it beside the animal while you briskly comb the hair coat with your fingers. If your pet has fleas, small pieces of flea "dirt" will be dislodged, producing a visible red bloodstain on the moist paper.

A few fleas can cause serious disease, and large numbers of fleas can cause significant loss of blood – especially in very young, very old or weakened animals. In fact, this blood loss can result in death – particularly in young puppies.

Fleas can survive off the host for months without obtaining a meal of blood. Feeding stimulates egg laying. Eggs hatch into larvae anywhere from two days to two weeks after laying. Mature flea larvae look similar to very small fly maggots and are found in cracks in floors, under carpets, pet bedding, baseboards and similar locations. After a little feeding, the larvae spins a cocoon in which they develop into adult fleas. Larvae take anywhere from ten days to several months to become adult fleas; it depends on the environmental conditions.

Because a major part of the flea's life cycle is spent away from pets (and for every flea on your canine there are probably numerous other fleas nearby), you cannot hope to control or alleviate a flea problem by simply treating your dog. Using an insecticide to kill fleas in the areas your dog frequents is crucial. Before using the insecticide, vacuum the house and dispose of the contents outside, in the garbage, tightly wrapped. Next, spray the areas frequented by your pet(s). These areas include pet bedding, carpeting, baseboards, furniture your pet uses, as well as other places used by your pet, both inside and outside the house. Make sure you follow the instructions on the insecticide carefully. Keep pets away from areas sprayed with the insecticide for several days.

There are numerous ways to treat fleas on a dog – everything from flea sprays to powders to shampoos to collars. Flea collars are designed to deal only with mild flea infestations. Make sure the collar is loose fitting (be able to insert two fingers between the collar and neck). A tightly applied flea collar can produce a zone of acute inflammation around the neck of some dogs. In general, flea collars are not very effective.

Some flea shampoos work. As well, there are a variety of sprays and powders available. Since flea sprays, powders, collars and most shampoos contain a variety of insecticides, be sure to follow the directions very carefully. Because insecticides are toxic, any flea control program should be carefully discussed with your veterinarian before being implemented. This includes asking your veterinarian's advice on what products and methods to use, how and when the products should be applied, and what to watch for. Ensure your own and your dog's safety.

Life Cycle of the Flea

25. Canine Heartworm

This serious disease, caused by the filarial worm, is common in the United States – particularly among mature dogs kept outside in mosquito-infested areas. But, it has moved north and is now found among canines in Canada. These worms can injure and kill dogs.

Adult worms live primarily in the right ventricle and the pulmonary artery near the heart. Heartworms are large, parasitic roundworms that feed on nutrients in the dog's bloodstream. Adult female heartworms are approximately twenty-seven centimetres long; adult male heartworms attain a length of approximately seventeen centimetres.

Immature worms, known as microfilariae, are discharged into the bloodstream by the female heartworms. Microfilariae remain active in the bloodstream for up to three years and only develop further when ingested by mosquitoes.

Within the mosquito, microfilariae develop into larvae.

Heartworms recovered from a dog.

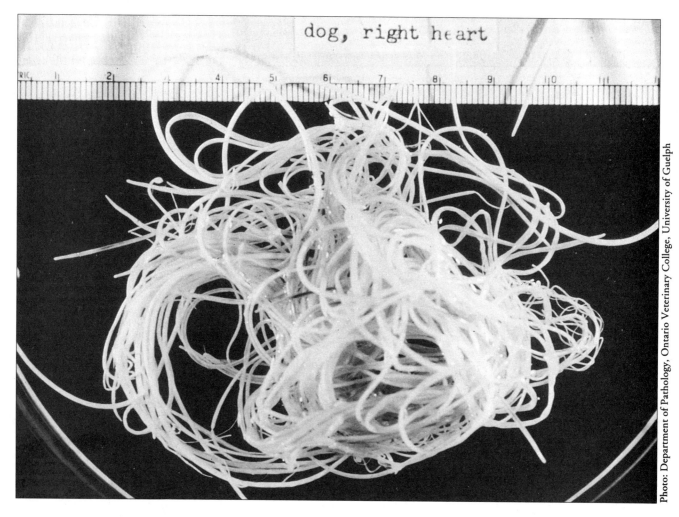

Photo: Department of Pathology, Ontario Veterinary College, University of Guelph

This process takes approximately two weeks. The larvae then migrate to the mouth parts of the mosquito from where it gains entrance into the dog when the mosquito feeds again.

Once inside the dog's tissue, the larvae develops, for approximately two months, before migrating to the right ventricle. The immature stages reach the right ventricle two to four months after infection. Worms reach maturity in another two to three months. Mature female worms begin producing microfilariae. Hence, microfilariae first appear approximately six months after infection.

Adult heartworms impair the flow of blood. This, in turn, can cause damage to the heart, lungs and liver. As well, fluid may build up in the lungs, impairing the dog's breathing.

A dog suffering from heartworm may show some of the following signs: gradual weight loss, decreased exercise tolerance, coughing, laboured breathing, listlessness and periodic collapsing.

Often dogs have suffered significant damage by the time outward signs are evident. For this reason, it is better to prevent heartworm disease, as opposed to treating it after infection.

The first step in prevention is to have your veterinarian do a blood test to see if your dog is infected. Infected dogs can be treated successfully. However, treatment can be costly and is potentially dangerous to your pet.

If your dog is not infected, it can be put on a preventative program as recommended by a veterinarian. A preventative program must not be started before your veterinarian determines that the dog does not have heartworm. Heartworm prevention usually lasts the entire time mosquitoes are present. These are the nasty insects that spread the disease.

26. Heat Stroke

In summer, dogs become very susceptible to heat stroke, and they may become fatalities if their guardians neglect them. These people do not use common sense and protect their canine companions during the "dog days of summer." Learn how your pet can suffer from heat stroke and protect your "best friend" from potentially harmful situations.

Dogs kept in hot, poorly ventilated places, especially without water, are likely to suffer from heat stroke. Short-nosed breeds such as Boxers, Pekingese and Bulldogs, to name but three, are particularly vulnerable.

One of the most common situations where dogs suffer (and often die) from heat stroke is when they are left in parked cars in warm weather. Temperatures inside a parked, poorly ventilated car can rapidly reach well over 100°F (38°C) on a relatively mild day during the summer, even if the car is parked in the shade.

Another common cause is to leave dogs tied up in a shadeless area for extended periods. A dog may initially be in a shaded area but be in direct sunlight later. Keep this in mind, and ensure the dog always has plenty of fresh water, in a non-spillable bowl. People often leave their dogs tied up all day, with no water, or water may be left but is spilt or becomes warm. As well, realize that dogs that have access to water and shade can still suffer from the heat.

Dogs enclosed in rooms or small buildings can be overcome by the heat. Ensure adequate ventilation, protection from the sun and plenty of fresh water.

Animals suffering from heat stroke show some of the following signs: exaggerated panting, increased pulse rate, anxious or staring expression, salivating; their tongues and lips look red (eventually may take on a bluish colour); there may be weakness, lack of coordination or even convulsions. Vomiting is also common. If the pet's temperature is allowed to continue to climb, the animal will collapse, go into a coma and die.

If you suspect your pet is suffering from heat stroke, it is vital to begin immediate treatment. First, remove the dog from the hot surroundings. Next, lower the dog's temperature by applying cold water to the animal's skin. The dog can be immersed up to its head in cold water. If this is not possible, spray your pet with cold water, especially on the groin. Let the dog rest in a cool place with some drinking water. Seek immediate veterinary attention.

While knowing what to do if your dog (or someone else's) suffers from heat stroke is very important, "prevention is the best medicine." Always carry water with you on hot days and give your dog small amounts frequently. Never put your pet in a situation where it could suffer from the heat.

If you see people putting their pet in potentially dangerous situations, take the time to educate them politely and inform them of what they should do to protect their pet. Do not think, "It is none of my business." Animal welfare is everyone's responsibility.

One of the most common situations where dogs suffer (and often die) from heat stroke is when they are left in a parked car in warm weather.

A Dog
for Life

Photo: N. Glenn Perrett

27. Involve Your Dog In Family Festivities

Family activities and holidays are special events that should be enjoyed by the whole family – four-legged family members included. All too often people ignore their pets during these family functions.

Christmas is a magical time of year, and is usually happy, if not hectic. However, it can be an unhappy, trying time for your pet: while people are enjoying themselves at parties and other social gatherings and events, their canine friend is forgotten.

Set aside some time each day to walk your dog. This will not only please your canine friend, but will also give you a little time to unwind from all the seasonal activities. An evening jaunt with your dog will provide both of you with exercise, and you can enjoy all the Christmas lights and decorations.

Sharing some play time benefits both you and your pet. Buy your pet some safe toys and participate in its enjoyment of these toys. Give it treats. Spoil it a little. After all, it is Christmas!

If you treat your pet to small portions of turkey or chicken, be sure the animal does not get any bones. Turkey and chicken bones are very brittle and tend to splinter, often lodging in the animal's throat or intestine. Portions of these foods should be kept small so as not to upset your pet's digestive system.

While some treats, given in moderation, are usually acceptable, dogs on restricted or prescription diets should only be given treats allowed by the animal's veterinarian.

If toys are purchased, make sure they are safe. In general, soft plastic toys that are easily chewed apart and "squeaky" toys where the squeaker is easily removed should be avoided. Any toys containing parts that are easily removed and swallowed are dangerous to pets. Balls that can be swallowed should also be off limits to your canine. Check with your veterinarian as well as qualified pet store employees to see what toys are appropriate for your dog.

(Opposite) Don't forget your dog during family festivities.

Christmas can be an exhausting time of year. When you need some rest, curl up on the couch with your canine friend and "catch forty winks." It is not necessary to spend the holidays amusing your pet, just spend time with it. This includes some "quiet time."

The holiday season (and times for other family gatherings) usually brings with it a hectic atmosphere. Changes in the day-to-day routine may unsettle your dog. Spending a little more time with your pet should alleviate some of the stress or added excitement your pet may be experiencing.

Holidays are a happy time. Enjoy them, but include your dog in your schedule. Remember, Christmas is a time for goodwill to all creatures.

28. When and Where to Board Your Pet

People who have a canine family member are usually faced, at one time or another, with the prospect of having to board their pet. This can be a difficult decision for the animal's guardian, and it will also likely result in a somewhat stressful situation for the dog.

The questions of when and where must be answered – but there are many variables involved. To the question "When?" I would answer "Only when necessary!" Separating a dog from the people it loves and trusts can be extremely stressful for the animal. The stress will likely be greater if the animal is to be kept in a confined and/or hectic atmosphere with other animals.

If you have to board your dog, take the time to check that the place is not only well suited for your animal, but is also acceptable to you. Who can best look after your pet depends on a variety of factors: how long you have to board your pet, how old and/or healthy the animal is, how well it copes with other animals, new environments, etc. These considerations (and others) should be carefully taken into account before choosing the best people (and facilities) to care for your pet. The following are some common choices for boarding dogs, with some of their advantages and disadvantages.

Caring for the Dog in its Home

There are obvious advantages if a responsible friend or family member cares for your dog in your home. Numerous people opt for this method because it is usually convenient, inexpensive (most friends are willing to do it for free – or in return for you minding their pets when they have to go away) and, most importantly, it is likely to be considerably less stressful for your pet than if it was boarded elsewhere. Whoever the person is, he or she should be willing to go to your home two or three times each day to ensure your dog is fed, watered, walked, spent time with and generally cared for until you return.

If the responsible person selected can stay in your home until you return, so much the better. In this way, the animal will be less likely to be lonely. Many relatives and friends don't mind a change of scenery for a while – especially if there are some comforts provided, starting with a well-stocked fridge!

Caring for the Dog in Someone Else's Home

Having trustworthy relatives or friends care for your pet in their home can also be an efficient way to board your pet. If the animal is familiar with and likes the people it is staying with, stress is less likely. You will probably feel less anxious, too, leaving your pet with people you know and trust, compared to strangers. Boarding your pet with relatives or friends can be an economical solution. Often the "service" may not cost you anything – except to return the favour sometime.

If you know the people, you are more likely to be able to leave specific and thorough instructions – and feel relatively sure that they will be carried out. As well, you will know that your pet will be cared for in a familiar manner, including being fed the same food. You can also try to have your pet's schedule adhered to as closely as possible. If your dog is fed and taken for walks at certain times of the day, you can try to have these activities maintained as close to "on-schedule" as possible. This can reduce some of the stress your pet will be experiencing from the absence of its family and its unfamiliar surroundings.

Generally speaking, having trustworthy relatives or friends care for your dog in their home, while you are away, is an efficient way of looking after your pet. Although the pet is in unfamiliar surroundings, it should have more company than if it were left at home and visited a couple of times a day. As well, this is probably a less stressful solution than boarding your pet at some kennels.

Professional "Pet Sitters"

If you want to keep your dog at home but do not know anyone who can care for your pet properly, you could contact a reputable company to look after your dog while you are away. Some of these people offer to stay at your house or to visit daily to care for your pet.

If you decide to hire such a service, ask for references or check the company out. Ask your veterinarian, friends, or the local humane society to recommend any good "pet sitters" or, just as important, name any bad ones to avoid. You don't want to leave your "best friend" with just anyone!

Boarding Facilities

If you can't leave your dog at home or with friends, you may decide to board it at some kennel. As with most things, there are excellent and terrible kennels – and everything in between. So, check out several facilities before deciding on where your pet will stay while you are away; ask other people you trust for recommendations; and, besides meeting the people who operate boarding facilities, you should also check a variety of other things:
• How do the indoor kennels compare to other kennels? Are they clean? Are they well ventilated?
• Are there adequate outdoor runs? Are the runs safe and well constructed so that your pet can't escape?
• Is the environment in which your pet will be staying pleasant or is it dirty, noisy, stressful, etc.?
• Do you get a good feeling about the kennels and the people who are operating them?

Don't be afraid to ask how often your dog will be taken for a walk, as well as what else they will do for it. Ask if they will feed your pet the food it is used to. If they do not have that brand, ask if you can leave them an adequate supply so that your dog can maintain its diet while you are away. The pooch will have enough to get used to, it does not need to change foods as well! Leave instructions as to how much food your dog receives. A good boarding facility should be willing to make your pet's stay as comfortable as possible.

Because there is always a significant risk of your dog acquiring a contagious disease when it frequents places exposed to large numbers of canines, ensure that it is up to date with its vaccinations. You should also make sure that the kennel only accepts pets that have been adequately immunized. Since puppies have not built up much of an immune system, even if they have received all of their vaccinations, they are especially susceptible to disease. So be particularly careful of where and when you board immature canines.

Just as your dog runs the risk of contracting a disease in a facility that boards pets, it can also acquire fleas. Good boarding facilities use sanitary procedures to reduce the presence of disease and fleas, but there is always a risk. After boarding your pet you should check it for fleas. If it appears not to have any – great. However, if there are indications that your dog acquired fleas while it was being boarded, you should treat it prior to taking it home. (To test, see Chapter 24.) Many boarding facilities will give your pet a "flea bath" just prior to your return, provided the dog is of adequate age.

Veterinary Clinics

Some veterinary clinics offer boarding services. Depending on the size of the animal hospital and the facilities they allocate for boarding animals, these establishments can be similar to regular boarding kennels. Again, there is often the stressful environment that comes with housing animals in cages and indoor runs. The barking alone can intimidate many dogs and result in a less-than-relaxing stay for your pet.

As with boarding kennels, dogs staying in veterinary clinics run the risk of being infected with disease or acquiring fleas. However, with proper disinfecting procedures, this risk can be greatly reduced.

Before leaving your dog at a veterinary clinic, ask to see how it will be cared for, where it will be staying and how often it will be walked each day. Remember, the primary function of a veterinary clinic is to provide health care for animals – boarding is a secondary function. Having said that, some veterinary hospitals take excellent care of the boarded animals. And this makes sense, especially if their next guest is a client!

The obvious advantage to leaving your pet at a veterinary clinic while you are away is that it can be taken care of if it gets sick. You might want to schedule some procedures your dog requires anyway, while it is being boarded – nail clipping, grooming, teeth cleaning, bathing, vaccinating and neutering (if any of these are required or desired).

Leave a phone number with the people at the veterinary hospital in case something does arise which needs tending to. Boarding your dog at your veterinarian's clinic can be a good idea because you already have a doctor/client relationship established and the people there should already be familiar with your pet and have its medical records should the animal become sick or injured.

Things To Remember When Boarding

No matter who looks after your pet, make sure they are responsible, are able to care for your pet properly, and that they will follow your instructions. Occasionally, call your "pet sitter" to ensure that your dog is alright. As well, leave a phone number where you can be reached should an emergency arise. Also leave the phone numbers of other people who can be phoned if an urgent situation occurs. Make sure you provide the phone number of the animal hospital and also the "after hours" emergency number. Also, leave the phone numbers of other family members and friends who can provide help if called upon. Just because you are away from your dog does not mean you are not responsible for it.

29. How to Reduce the Stress of Moving

The anxiety and general uneasiness experienced during the moving process not only affects people but also animals. To reduce the stress and bewilderment many pets experience, they should be comforted with extra attention and affection.

When Lynn, I, and our canine companions, moved a few years ago, Lynn and I coped, but the dogs did considerably better making an efficient and quick adjustment to their new surroundings. This is somewhat surprising. We had not only lived out of boxes for several months, but we also had to conduct some immediate renovations, which added to the already hectic atmosphere.

What made the transition easier was that we were able to move into our new home gradually. To get our dogs used to their new home, we took a dog or two for short visits to their new premises. Having made a few visits prior to moving day, the dogs were not overwhelmed.

The fact that I came down with a bad case of the flu the day after moving also made adjusting to a new place easier for the dogs. While I was in no shape to walk the dogs or play with them, I was there to help them adapt to their new surroundings. Apparently dogs are considerably more adaptable than I am!

While some dogs adjust well to change, many pets do not. A period of adjustment may be needed by a pet during a move or other significant change. This adjustment period can be made easier for your pet if you give it a little more attention and affection. Do not spoil it; just be there for it, in case it feels somewhat "lost" for the first while.

We tried to keep our dogs' routine in the new house similar to how it was in the old house. A major difference, however, was that our new house did not have a fenced-in yard. So, unlike our other house, we could not let the dogs outside. To make up for this, we had to walk the dogs two or three times a day. This was difficult in the beginning, when I had the flu. Lynn was responsible for walking all the dogs (at that time we had seven) for the first few weeks.

Each pet responds to change in its own way. Some animals take a while to get acclimatized to the change; others make the transition as if nothing had happened. Whether your dog handles changes well or not, it is important to be sympathetic to your pet during these times. Spend as much time with it as possible and do things that will enable your dog to become accustomed to the change quickly and easily.

30. Responsibility and the Aging Dog

Brandy, our aging Wirehaired Fox Terrier and constant companion for over a decade, had been significantly slowing down. At age thirteen or fourteen, she had every right to do so. (Brandy was young but fully grown when she was found as a stray, so her exact age was not known. After unsuccessful attempts to locate the owners, Brandy became a welcome and spirited addition to the family.)

During her last couple of years, the aging process had a dramatic effect on Brandy. Her sight and hearing deteriorated to the point where she was, to all intents and purposes, blind and deaf. This occasionally left our friend disoriented.

Although it hurt us to see Brandy drift away from the energetic dog she once was, Lynn and I did take some comfort knowing that Brandy was coping with growing old and adjusting accordingly. Both Brandy and I realized that her days of running around the fenced-in backyard were gone. The majority of her days were spent sleeping or resting. Even when she slept, Brandy was less active than in her younger days. She now "chased fewer rabbits."

Growing old not only limited Brandy physically, but also made her increasingly dependent. Besides relying on us occasionally for direction, Brandy also relied on us to clean up any of her unfortunate accidents. No longer could Brandy be relied upon not to relieve herself in the house for periods of twelve hours. If we went out of the house for longer than a few hours, there was a good chance that we would have some cleaning to do later.

Another minor inconvenience we experienced with

(Opposite) As Brandy aged she slept a lot. Here she sleeps with Nanaimo.

Photo: N. Glenn Perrett

Brandy's aging was that she needed to be fed a special diet, consisting of a no-salt dog food. To this we added some vitamins prescribed by our veterinarian. While this special diet was not a major problem, it cost a little more in both time and money.

Brandy was now considerably more restricted in her activities than she had been a couple of years prior; she needed more care and created slightly more work for Lynn and myself. However, we never considered having her "put to sleep" until we were sure that she was experiencing pain, with no hope of a cure or adequate recovery, or that she could not get any further enjoyment out of life. Since this latter reason is based on personal judgement, I don't consider euthanasia except in extreme cases and then only after getting a similar opinion from a veterinarian.

Brandy was still enjoying getting out for short walks as well as eating, although her appetite had decreased. Her presence and quiet companionship (Brandy's loss of sight and hearing lessened her, as with many Terriers, tremendous barking capacity) were still cherished. We knew that when the time came when Brandy was no longer physically part of our lives there would be a large empty space that Lynn and I would somehow have to deal with.

* * *

Unfortunately, many dogs are not allowed to continue living once they have significantly "slowed down" or have become a "burden." On more than one occasion, I have heard people say that they had to put their dog "down" because the dog could no longer control its bodily functions. These and other equally feeble excuses are usually stated in a way that make it sound as if the dog was actually suffering. While this occasionally is the case, often it is not. Frequently the dog experiences nothing more than a little embarrassment from creating these minor incidents. Often, upon being "caught in the act," the dog will look as if to say, "I know I am old enough to know better but I just could not help it."

(Opposite) Here Brandy sleeps on top of Nanaimo!

Many people believe that having their dog "put to sleep" when old age sets in, or some other minor inconvenience occurs, is for the good of the dog. Others have their dog destroyed simply because the poor pooch has become more work than it once was. These people usually "solve" the problem in the most convenient way for themselves – by having the animal killed.

This is not to say that there is no place for euthanasia for dogs. On the contrary, there are numerous reasons to end a dog's life humanely. A dog should not have to suffer significantly, without any hope of having the suffering alleviated or, at the very least, reduced. On the other hand, a dog should not have its life shortened to suit the convenience of its guardian(s).

Raising and properly caring for a dog is a tremendous responsibility. This should not be taken on until all aspects have been carefully considered. Too often, a puppy or dog is purchased on a whim, without any thought given as to what good dog care entails. Food, shelter, love, veterinary care and quality time spent with the dog by its guardian(s) are some of the bare necessities that should be provided. However, raising a dog responsibly also includes "sacrifices" – which are a dog's right. One of these rights includes the chance to a full and happy life. Obviously, if the dog's health is failing and causing significant suffering to the animal, with no chance of this suffering being cured or adequately lessened, then it is necessary to have the animal "put to sleep." However, it is not appropriate to have the animal killed as a matter of convenience.

* * *

Shortly after Brandy had been put on a special diet, Lynn and I had the difficult decision of whether to have Brandy "put to sleep" or not. From a medical point of view, the decision was not a difficult one. In a matter of a few weeks, Brandy had developed a malignant tumour that stretched across the width of her abdomen and was pushing on her bowels. Our veterinarian's prognosis was that Brandy had only a few days left and although she had not suffered, she was beginning to experience some discomfort. This, combined with the fact that Brandy's condition had quickly deteriorated during the last few days to the point where she lost her balance, was very weak and ate very little, made choosing the proper thing only a matter of uttering our actual consent.

Although Dr. St. John was very confident that the problem was cancer and that nothing could be done, he did an x-ray to satisfy Lynn and me as well as himself. After Brandy was euthanized, an autopsy was done to confirm what was already known and to further reassure us that putting Brandy to sleep was not only the right thing to do, but the only humane solution.

As it turned out, Brandy not only had a large tumour on her spleen, but also had numerous smaller tumours. All of this did convince us that we had taken the only option. Removing doubt made the difficult decision a little easier, and for that we are extremely grateful to Dr. St. John. It seems appropriate that the same person who had found Brandy as a stray all those years ago and who had skillfully tended to her medical needs was the one who caringly ended her life at the appropriate time.

Knowing we had made the right choice did nothing to fill the empty space we felt. The empty space is smaller now, and while time may diminish its size, it will never go away completely. For several days following Brandy's death, Lynn and I would hear our faithful friend barking, or we would catch a glimpse of her for a fleeting moment. Physically, Brandy is no longer with us; however, fond thoughts and memories of her are, and she will continue to be part of our lives. While Brandy cannot be replaced, the space she occupied has been filled by several canines in need of a good home.

(Opposite) Brandy – lovingly remembered.

(Below) Brandy sleeps on a bed made for her by Lynn.

Photo: N. Glenn Perrett

31. Deceased Pets and Fond Memories

The death of a pet can be an extremely painful and trying time for its guardians. Grieving for a beloved pet is different for each person. Some people grieve for a short period of time; others take much longer. Some people go right out and acquire another pet. Some wait much longer. Others never again share their lives with a pet. Whatever the case, it is important to remember the good times and the special bond that existed.

The fact that Brandy had had a long and happy life was of little comfort to Lynn and me, at the time. After losing Brandy, our immediate feelings centered on the fact that we had lost a dear friend. But Brandy was more than a close friend, she was a cherished family member; always there for us. Our love for Brandy was only surpassed by her unswerving loyalty and affection for us. I felt terrible when Brandy died, as I had when Chips, our Beagle, died many years ago.

Most of the sadness Lynn and I felt when we lost Brandy is gone. Occasionally we remember Brandy with sadness, because she's not around, but most of our memories are happy ones. She lived a happy and long life.

A common mistake people make in acquiring a pet after their other pet died is comparing the two animals. I have often heard people say that their current pet is nice but it will never replace their other pet. Many people refuse to get another pet, believing they will never find another pet as "good" as the one they had. It is unfair to compare pets, and a new pet should not be acquired to replace the old pet.

No other animal will be the same as the pet that preceded it. Some of its characteristics may be similar, but the two pets will be different – no matter what. As with people, all animals are unique – in appearance and personality. Treat each pet as an individual, realizing it has many good qualities (maybe the occasional minor fault). Don't compare it to other pets.

One of the few drawbacks to sharing your life with a dog is that you will probably outlive your canine companion. Dealing with the death of a faithful friend is difficult under any circumstances. The positive side of having a longer lifespan than dogs is that you can share your life, if you choose, with many canines.

Gandhi said, "The greatness of a nation can be judged by the way its animals are treated." While all nations are guilty of exploiting animals on a large scale, more and more people are becoming sympathetic and caring towards animals.

Anyone who has experienced the special relationship that exists between humans and pets knows how important these creatures are to our way of life and even to our existence. People can learn a tremendous amount from animals. While dogs do not live as long as we would like, fond memories of them last a lifetime.

A Final Word

I love dogs. There is no friendlier, more caring, loyal species on this planet. The dog's honourable character and giving nature is unsurpassed by any other animal – including *Homo sapiens*.

However, as fond as I am of canines, there is a part of me that wishes that these animals had not been domesticated thousands of years ago. Having made dogs dependent on us, we have failed them miserably.

Yes, many people treat their dogs well – with great respect and care. These people do not see their canines as possessions or status symbols but rather as family members.

Unfortunately, a substantial number of people don't honour the basic standards of pet care. Dogs are commonly neglected, abused, abandoned and generally treated very poorly. As well, many irresponsible people allow their dogs to breed. This indiscriminate breeding results in literally thousands of friendly, loving dogs having to be killed daily in North America.

For every dog sleeping comfortably in the living room with its human family members, there are numerous others leading a lonely existence. Many of these unfortunate canines are kept outdoors, where they receive little in the way of companionship. Still others are abandoned, abused or neglected.

We should be kind to all living creatures. This is particularly true of those animals we have domesticated and, in the process, have made dependent on us. Dogs, with their innocent and giving ways, should be treated humanely.

If you currently share your life with a canine, ensure it is well cared for. If you are considering acquiring a dog, do not do so until you are sure that you are ready for the responsibility of properly raising the animal for its entire life. Dogs are considerably more than "pets," they are sentient creatures deserving of our love, respect, care, admiration and all the good things in life that we can give them.

The dog's honourable character and giving nature is unsurpassed by any other animal.

Appendix A: Common Poisonous Plants

Plant	Toxic Parts	Plant Type
Aconite	roots, foliage, seeds	garden flower
Apple	seeds	cultivated tree
Arrowgrasses	leaves	marsh plants
Atropa belladonna	entire plant esp. seeds, roots	garden herb
Autumn Crocus	entire plant	garden flower
Azaleas	entire plant	cultivated & wild shrub
Baneberry	berries, roots	wildflower
Bird-of-Paradise	pods	garden flower
Black Locust	entire plant esp. bark, shoots	tree
Bloodroot	entire plant esp. stem, roots	wildflower, herb
Box	entire plant esp. leaves	ornamental shrub
Buckeye	sprouts, nuts, seeds	tree
Buttercup	entire plant esp. leaves	wildflower, garden herb
Caladium	entire plant	house plant
Carolina jessamine	flowers, leaves	ornamental plant
Castor bean	entire plant esp. beans	house plant
Chinaberry tree	berries	tree
Chokecherries	leaves, cherries, pit	wild shrub
Christmas berry	leaves	shrub
Christmas Rose	rootstock, leaves	garden flower
Common privet	leaves, berries	ornamental shrub
Corn cockle	seeds	wildflower, weed
Cowbane	entire plant esp. roots	wildflower, herb
Cow cockle	seeds	wildflower, weed
Cowslip	entire plant esp. leaves, stem	wildflower, herb
Daffodil	bulbs	garden flower
Daphne	bark, berries, leaves	ornamental shrub
Death Camas	leaves, stems, seeds, flowers	field herb
Delphinium (Larkspur)	entire plant esp. sprouts	wildflower
Dumbcane	entire plant	house plant
Dutchman's breeches	roots, foliage	wild & garden flower
Elderberry	leaves, bark, roots, buds	tree
Elephant's ear	entire plant	house plant
English Ivy	entire plant esp. leaves, berries	ornamental vine
European Bittersweet	entire plant esp. berries	vine
False Flax	seeds	wild herb
False hellebore	roots, leaves, seeds	ornamental flower
Fan weed	seeds	wildflower, herb
Field peppergrass	seeds	wildflower, herb
Flax	seed-pods	wildflower, herb
Foxglove	leaves	wild & garden flower
Holly	berries	shrub
Horsechestnut	nuts, sprouts	tree
Horse nettle	entire plant esp. berries	wildflower, herb
Hyacinth	bulbs	wild & house plant
Iris	leaves, roots	wild & garden flower
Jack-in-the-pulpit	entire plant esp. roots, leaves	wildflower

Plant	Toxic Parts	Plant Type
Jatropha	seeds	tree, shrub
Jerusalem Cherry	unripe fruit, foliage	ornamental plant
Jimsonweed	entire plant esp. seeds	field plant
Laburnum	seeds, pods, flowers	ornamental plant
Lantana	foliage	house plant
Larkspur	young plants	wildflower
Laurels	leaves	shrub
Lily of the valley	leaves, flowers	garden & wildflower
Lupines	seeds, pods	shrub
Manchineel Tree	sap, fruit	tree
Matrimony vine	leaves, shoots	ornamental vine
Mayapple	unripe fruit, roots, foliage	wildflower
Milk vetch	entire plant	wildflower
Mistletoe	berries	house plant
Monkshood	entire plant esp. roots, seeds	wildflower
Moonseed	fruit, roots	vine
Morning glory	seeds, roots	wildflower
Mountain mahogany	leaves	shrub
Mustards	seeds	wildflower
Narcissus	bulbs	garden flower
Nicotiana	leaves	garden flower
Nightshade	leaves, berries	wildflower, vine
Oaks	shoots, leaves	tree
Oleander	leaves	ornamental shrub
Philodendron	entire plant	house plant
Pokeweed	roots, seeds, berries,	field plant
Poinsettia	leaves, stem, flowers	house plant
Poison hemlock	leaves, stem, fruit	field plant
Potato	shoots, sprouts	garden plant
Rattle box	entire plant	wildflower
Rhododendron	leaves	ornamental shrub
Rhubarb	leaves	garden plant
Rosary pea	seeds	house plant
Skunk cabbage	entire plant esp. roots, leaves	marsh plant
Smartweeds	sap	wildflower
Snow-on-the-mountain	sap	field plant
Sorghum	leaves	grass
Star of Bethlehem	entire plant	wildflower
Velvet grass	leaves	grass
Wild black cherry	leaves, pits	tree
Wild radish	seeds	wildflower
Wisteria	pods, seeds	ornamental plant
Woody aster	entire plant	wildflower
Yellow jessamine	entire plant	ornamental vine
Yellow oleander	entire plant esp. leaves	garden plant
Yellow pine flax	entire plant esp. seed-pods	wildflower
Yew	bark, leaves, seeds	ornamental tree

Acknowledgements

Many people were instrumental in the preparation of *A Dog For Life: The Practical Guide to Canine Care*. I would particularly like to extend my thanks to the following:

Dr. P. K. St. John (my cousin and trusted and skilled veterinarian) for providing me with helpful information and insight and who generously wrote "A Veterinarian's Note";

R. D. Lawrence, who kindly wrote the "Foreword" and who has given me valuable advice;

Tony Hawke, for giving me my first opportunity to have a published book;

Dennis Mills, for editing my writing;

Gerard Williams, for his creativity;

John Rutledge, for his patience and artistic eye while photographing our dogs;

My family (including my brother Neil whose illustrations greatly enhance my written thoughts) for their constant and much appreciated support;

Lynn, not only for her love and patience, but also for her valued opinions and proofreading skills; and

To all the dogs I have had the pleasure of meeting. It is these wonderful creatures who gave me the inspiration to put my thoughts and beliefs to paper. It is through this book that I hope to return some of the many positive things they have given me.

Additional Credits

Front Cover Photo Key

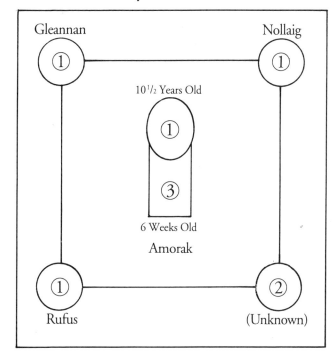

Gleannan   Nollaig

10 ½ Years Old

6 Weeks Old

Amorak

Rufus   (Unknown)

1 John Rutledge
2 N. Glenn Perrett
3 Norman W. Perrett

Illustrations

Neil Perrett is an artist and a teacher who lives in Elora, Ontario.

Page 1 The author grew up with Chips, the first family pet.
Page 23 Accommodating the author's life with dogs meant constructing a fence for them.
Page 33 Many outdoor dogs lead a lonely existence.
Page 41 Walking your dog will provide exercise for both of you.
Page 59 Providing Brandy with a bed made her "golden years" more comfortable.
Page 69 Amorak at six weeks, and ten and a half years of age.

Health Record

Name _____

Breed _____ Sex _____

Markings _____

Date of Birth _____

Date of Neuter _____
(Spay/Castration)

Veterinarian _____

Veterinarian
Hospital _____

Address _____

Phone ( ) _____

Emergency Phone ( ) _____

Important Phone Numbers and Addresses

_____

_____

_____

_____

_____

Medical and Other Relevant Information (Medications, Treatments, etc.)

_____

_____

_____

_____

_____

_____

_____

_____

_____

_____

_____

Vaccination Record

Date	Vaccinated For	Date	Vaccinated For

Heartworm Tests

Date	Result	Comments

Fecal Tests

Date	Result	Comments

Health Record

Name _____

Breed _____ Sex _____

Markings _____

Date of Birth _____

Date of Neuter
(Spay/Castration) _____

Veterinarian _____

Veterinarian
Hospital _____

Address _____

Phone ( )

Emergency Phone ( )

Important Phone Numbers and Addresses

_____

_____

_____

_____

_____

Medical and Other Relevant Information (Medications, Treatments, etc.)

_____

_____

_____

_____

_____

_____

_____

_____

_____

_____

_____

Vaccination Record

Date	Vaccinated For		Date	Vaccinated For
_____	_____		_____	_____
_____	_____		_____	_____
_____	_____		_____	_____
_____	_____		_____	_____
_____	_____		_____	_____
_____	_____		_____	_____
_____	_____		_____	_____
_____	_____		_____	_____
_____	_____		_____	_____

Heartworm Tests

Date	Result	Comments
_____	_____	_____
_____	_____	_____
_____	_____	_____
_____	_____	_____
_____	_____	_____
_____	_____	_____
_____	_____	_____
_____	_____	_____
_____	_____	_____
_____	_____	_____
_____	_____	_____
_____	_____	_____

Fecal Tests

Date	Result	Comments
_____	_____	_____
_____	_____	_____
_____	_____	_____
_____	_____	_____
_____	_____	_____
_____	_____	_____
_____	_____	_____
_____	_____	_____
_____	_____	_____
_____	_____	_____
_____	_____	_____
_____	_____	_____

Notes

Notes

Notes

Notes

Notes

Notes